the **NO-NONSENSE** guide to

INDIGENOUS PEOPLES

Lotte Hughes

'Publishers have created lists of short books that discuss the questions that your average [electoral] candidate will only ever touch if armed with a slogan and a soundbite. Together [such books] hint at a resurgence of the grand educational tradition... Closest to the hot headline issues are *The No-Nonsense Guides*. These target those topics that a large army of voters care about, but that politicos evade. Arguments, figures and documents combine to prove that good journalism is far too important to be left to (most) journalists.'

Boyd Tonkin,
The Independent,
London

The No-Nonsense Guide to Indigenous Peoples
Published in Canada by
New Internationalist Publications   and   Between the Lines
401 Richmond Street West   720 Bathurst Street
Studio 393   Suite 404
Toronto   Toronto
Ontario   Ontario
M5V 3A8   M5S 2R4
www.newint.org   **www.btlbooks.com**

First published in the UK by
New Internationalist™ Publications Ltd
Oxford OX4 1BW
New Internationalist is a registered trade mark.

This edition not to be sold outside Canada.

Cover image: Maasi man in Kenya. William Manning/Corbis.

Design by Alan Hughes/New Internationalist Publications Ltd.
Series editor: Troth Wells

Printed by TJ International Ltd, Padstow, Cornwall, UK.

National Library of Canada Cataloguing in Publication
Hughes, Lotte
The no-nonsense guide to indigenous peoples / Lotte Hughes

(The no-nonsense guides)
Includes bibliographical references and index.
ISBN 1-896357-76-8

1. Indigenous peoples. I. Title II. Series: No-nonsense guides (Toronto,
Ont.)

GN380.H83 2003   305.8   C2002-905779-5

the **NO-NONSENSE** guide to

INDIGENOUS PEOPLES

Lotte Hughes

160201

About the author

Lotte Hughes is a freelance journalist and historian, with a particular interest in the Maasai of East Africa and oral history. She recently finished a doctorate on Maasai colonial history, and her next project is researching the environmental history of the Commonwealth. She has travelled widely, written about development and human rights issues for newspapers and NGOs, and won the John Morgan Writing Award 1996/7. Co-author of *Interviewing children: A guide for journalists and others* (Save the Children UK, 1998).

Acknowledgements

Particular thanks go (in no particular order) to Mike Sansom, Maui Solomon, Gary Foley, Hugh Brody, Ken Hyder, Romeo Saganash, Caroline Gullick, Moronga Tanago, Willemien le Roux and other colleagues at WIMSA, Chris Low, Lyndon Ormond Parker, Ben Knighton, Eben Kirksey, Sue Wheat of Tourism Concern, Anette Molbech of IWGIA, Graham Fox of Minority Rights Group International, Beth Herzfeld, Jeff Howarth and Mike Kaye at Anti-Slavery International, Charles Swaisland, John Beauclerk, the Center for World Indigenous Studies, Chris Richards, Wayne Ellwood and Carolyn Brown. Many thanks to Tom Griffiths, of the Forest Peoples Programme, for checking and commenting on the manuscript. Also to my father, David Hughes, for his many insights and inputs.

The views expressed are not necessarily those of New Internationalist Publications Ltd or the author, but of the individuals and organizations quoted.

Other titles in the series:

The No-Nonsense Guide to Fair Trade
The No-Nonsense Guide to Globalization
The No-Nonsense Guide to Climate Change
The No-Nonsense Guide to International Migration
The No-Nonsense Guide to Sexual Diversity
The No-Nonsense Guide to World History
The No-Nonsense Guide to Class, Caste & Hierarchies
The No-Nonsense Guide to Democracy
The No-Nonsense Guide to International Development
The No-Nonsense Guide to The Arms Trade
The No-Nonsense Guide to Terrorism

Foreword

THE HISTORY OF THE WORLD is inseparable from the fate of indigenous peoples. From Australia to Amazonia, groups who occupied the fertile shores and river valleys have been pushed into far, infertile corners of their own worlds, or exterminated by explorers, colonizers and nation states. This means that the morality of our world is also bound up in their fate. How a 'modern' state views and deals with aboriginal peoples is revealing. The survivors may be in 'remote' arid, icy or hidden landscapes, but their significance lies at the center, not the periphery, of our world.

Lotte Hughes' remarkable book charts the histories and politics of indigenous societies. Some issues are complicated and unresolved: the notion of 'indigenous' is full of contention, with a maze of definitions. A strength of this *Guide* is that it acknowledges difficulties and refuses deconstruction, without obscuring the variety and complexity of indigenous societies.

The *Guide* describes the achievements, as well as the grief and oppression. It highlights the key feature of indigenous systems: a nurturing, respectful relationship to the land. Indigenous peoples wish to ensure that the land they use and the creatures they kill to eat will continue to sustain them. This is revealed in a fascinating intersection between religious and material relationships to the world. Many Europeans have taken inspiration from this, sometimes being derided as naïve and romantic. For indigenous peoples can be just as ruthless with their environment or with one another as the rest of us. In addressing romanticism, Lotte Hughes points out that indigenous societies need the world around them to stay the same: survival depends on the land and animals remaining as they are, with only minor changes. To note this is not to romanticize but to report social and economic realities. Environmental conservatism does not make people 'good', or mean they are without human cruelties – but it does mean that they have tended to be good environmentalists. It also means that they have expertise that can benefit not just local territories, but all peoples.

The success of their environmentalism makes their displacement all the more poignant. For loss of land usually means the loss of the possibility to be themselves. They rely on the territory: where ancestors have nurtured the earth, cared for the animals, propitiated the spirits. A cruel irony of their displacement is that they have often been accused, by those wishing to displace them, of killing too many animals, over-fishing or neglecting the land. Hence many groups have been forced out of national parks in East and southern Africa, despite having ensured, by their customs and skills, the enduring beauty and abundance of these places. Elsewhere, mines, forestry and intensive agriculture have dispossessed so many.

But this *Guide* also tells of the fight back. Indigenous groups have formed international alliances, and have a permanent presence at the UN. They are battling to secure rights to live on their lands, to check logging, to preserve fisheries, to manage their own resources and to take effective part in government. These struggles may be versions of David and Goliath, without promise of miraculous outcome. But there have been successes. The challenge now is for indigenous peoples to define, and the rest of the world to respect, a development model that is neither an unrealistic ideal of times gone nor an acceptance of final assimilation in colonial nation states. Indigenous peoples ask that their voices be heard, their stories be told and that they take their place, on their own terms, in their own lands. This *No-Nonsense Guide* lays out the issues behind and within this challenge.

Hugh Brody
Anthropologist, film-maker and author of *Maps and Dreams* and *The Other Side of Eden*
London

the **NO-NONSENSE** guide to

INDIGENOUS PEOPLES

CONTENTS

Foreword by Hugh Brody 5

Introduction 8

1 Overview 10

2 Colonialism and conquest 29

3 Land and nature 46

4 Facing the problems 60

5 Fighting back 83

6 Music and magic 108

**7 Development, justice
and future challenges** 120

Contacts 139

Bibliography 141

Index 142

the ▐ **NO-NONSENSE** ▌ guide to

INDIGENOUS PEOPLES

IN AFRICA, a very old medicine man whom I was interviewing said to me – after asking my age (40-something, which felt bad enough) – 'Huh! When you're 70, that's when you will start getting the knowledge you were born with; it will start working on you. That's when you will start realizing that natural knowledge.' He was dismissing my comparative youth and the knowledge I had picked up in school and college, saying that I would in time tap into something deeper. I live in hope.

As a journalist and later as an historian doing fieldwork in Africa, indigenous people taught me a great deal and rightly challenged my ignorance. The only way a non-indigenous person should approach the whole subject is with humility and readiness to learn.

In my experience, indigenous peoples have many admirable qualities that are sorely needed in today's world – including spirituality, egalitarianism, a sense of being grounded or centered, a lack of neurosis, wisdom, strength, usually a great sense of humor and perspective, too. They foresaw the global social and environmental crisis generations ago, and it's about time the rest of us paid attention to their vision and example.

When I began to research this *No-Nonsense Guide*, the catalogue of horrors suffered by indigenous peoples seemed overwhelming. The chapters on colonialism and subsequent problems could have run and run. But although it is politically correct to talk about survivors rather than victims, this is truly the case with indigenous peoples. Often, too much emphasis is put upon victimization and not enough is said about the way people have fought back. Also, it seemed to me that there was too much romanticization in some of the literature, which does not do indigenous peoples any favors either – they are *not* 'noble savages'.

I have tried to strike a balance. The chapter on resistance describes the many forms indigenous struggle can take and celebrates some successes. Rather than paint a totally rosy picture of indigenous life, I have also mentioned tensions and contradictions. In recent years, new alliances in global networking have provided new openings for indigenous activism at international level. This is an exciting development, which is making indigenous peoples – so often regarded as 'marginalized' – more visible and audible. Above all, they demand the right to speak for themselves and I have tried to include, where possible, as many direct voices as I can.

But where do you start? All the communities mentioned in this book are worth a book or more in their own right. It is impossible to do justice in such a small space to all the people, historical milestones, ideas and events. All I can do is give illustrative snapshots, in the hope that readers will be inspired to find out more elsewhere. The many omissions must be put down to limited space, not oversight. The mistakes are all my own, for I have not yet got 'the knowledge'.

Lotte Hughes
Oxford

1 Overview

Some definitions and an overview... What is the difference between indigenous peoples, tribal peoples and minorities? Competing claims to indigenousness... Indigenous peoples and the United Nations... How many, and where and how they live.

A MIDDLE-AGED AMERICAN woman tourist and a young Maasai man bumped into each other at the entrance of a luxury hotel in Tanzania's Ngorongoro reserve. It was late 1983, and my Maasai friend Taté held a copy of George Orwell's novel *1984*, which he happened to be reading. He was dressed in a red toga-like garment (*shuka*) and adorned with beaded jewelry, looking every inch a 'man of the bush' – yet carrying a symbol of modernity and literacy.

The tourist timidly asked Taté in pidgin English, raising her camera: 'Can-I-take-your-picture?' My friend coolly looked her up and down. With some amusement he said, in perfect American-accented English acquired from American missionary teachers: 'Only if you are paying in US dollars, lady.' She fled, embarrassed, without taking a photo.

What does this exchange say about the way we often treat indigenous people? The tourist clearly assumed that Taté did not understand English. She did not notice the book, or perhaps not being a lover of litera-ture, maybe did not know what it was. She probably thought him decorative and exotic, and with the best will in the world, wanted to capture his picture to take home and show the folks (as perhaps many of us have done). It would end up alongside photos of lions and jungles, part of a gallery of images of wild Africa. He, meanwhile, had other ideas. Tourists are welcome in Ngorongoro because they bring much-needed money. But since Maasai communities were forced out of the crater some years ago to make way for tourism and 'conservation', they have not seen many direct benefits of either activity. They were, and are, fed up with being treated like human animals in a zoo – and widely seen as dumb and stupid, too. If she wanted his photo, he wanted to make a dollar on the deal. He thought the whole thing quite amusing; she was just confused. They were beings from completely different worlds, colliding in space and bruised by the collision. The story of indigenous peoples mirrors this one in many ways, but their struggle for recognition is usually much more serious, and the collision a lot more painful.

Who are indigenous peoples?

Indigenous peoples are generally referred to in the plural, because there are many different groups who make up the entire global tapestry of indigenous peoples. The use of plural indicates the diversity of people within the group as a whole.

People do not agree on definitions, and in fact there is no unambiguous definition of the concept. Indigenous peoples themselves claim the right to define who they are, and reject the idea that outsiders can do so. They argue that self-identification as indigenous is one of their basic rights. Nevertheless anthropologists, for example, tend to use the term indigenous peoples to describe a non-dominant group in a particular territory, with a more or less acknowledged claim to be aboriginal – a word now used (with an initial capital letter) for the indigenous peoples of Australia in particular. But in its broadest sense, aboriginal simply means 'original inhabitants'. They are

---

Indigenous, *a.* 1646. [f. L. *indigena* + -OUS; see prec.] **1.** Born or produced naturally in a land or region; native *to* (the soil, region, etc.). b. *transf.* and *fig.* Inborn, innate 1864. **2.** Native, vernacular 1844.
The Shorter Oxford English Dictionary.

the people who were there first, who may also call themselves First Peoples or First Nations.

The Aboriginal peoples of Australia were undoubtedly there first, and the same is true of other groups such as the Maya of Guatemala, Central America, and certain (some would say all) African peoples. But in some places the issue is not always so clear cut. Neither is it clear cut within Africa where, for example, nomadic migrants from the north of the continent displaced other early peoples from territories further south which the incomers later claimed as their ancestral lands. Though an indigenous people may have arrived in a particular territory before other ethnic groups, there is a problem with the word 'first'. In some cases, who knows who got there first? The history of the world is the story of human migration – successive waves of people moving here and there, displacing other populations as they moved, conquered and occupied new territory. When you start digging, as archaeologists have, you find that the terms 'original' and 'first' are not always strictly accurate. Other communities can claim to be first-comers, or to have arrived in the same region simultaneously. But some of those first-comers – like the Arawaks of the Caribbean island of Hispaniola – are now extinct, so they cannot speak for themselves.

It may be safer to say that indigenous peoples arrived in a territory before single nation states were formed, though to complicate matters this is equally true of some other communities who do not self-identify as indigenous, such as the Kikuyu of Kenya. Also, some indigenous peoples such as Native Americans were organized as sovereign nations long before European colonists arrived; for example, the Iroquois Confederacy comprised six nations and operated a highly structured state system.

However, these nations did not form single nation states as we know them today.[1] The International Work Group for Indigenous Affairs (IWGIA) gives this definition, as part of a longer one:

'Indigenous peoples are the disadvantaged descendants of those peoples that inhabited a territory prior to the formation of a state. The term indigenous may be defined as a characteristic relating the identity of a particular people to a particular area and distinguishing them culturally from other people or peoples. When, for example, immigrants from Europe settled in the Americas and Oceania, or when new states were created after colonialism was abolished in Africa and Asia, certain peoples became marginalized and discriminated against because their language, their religion, their culture and their whole way of life were different, and perceived by the dominant society as being inferior. Insisting on their right to self-determination is indigenous peoples' way of overcoming these obstacles. Today many indigenous peoples are still excluded from society and often even deprived of their rights as equal citizens of a state.'[2]

Indigenous peoples are often defined as 'non-state' and their mode of life and economy is not industrialized. This makes them vulnerable; they tend to be marginalized, which means pushed to the margins of society. This does not mean to say that individuals cannot be members of governments and parliaments, help to run the country, or work in factories. But generally speaking they are not at the head of things, running states and industry.

'Tribal peoples' can mean much the same thing. The major difference is that they do not or cannot always claim to be descended from the aboriginal inhabitants of a territory. Also, the word 'tribal', like 'tribe', can be insulting to some, and so is best avoided unless people choose to describe themselves this way. The word tribe is acceptable in the US, where it refers to a group of Native Americans who share a common language and culture, but is only acceptable in a few areas of Canada.

Many minorities are also indigenous, but not

necessarily so. Examples of minority groups who are indigenous are the Karen of Burma (Myanmar) and the Yanomami of Brazil. Examples of minorities who are not indigenous are Korean Americans, British Asians and Jehovah's Witnesses (unless individuals also happen to be members of indigenous groups). Surprisingly, there is no internationally agreed definition of minorities. The UN Declaration on Minorities covers 'national or ethnic, religious and linguistic' minorities, but in 50 years the UN has never agreed a definition of what constitutes a minority. The organization Minority Rights Group International (MRG) says minorities are 'often among the poorest and most marginalized groups in society. They may lack access to political power and frequently have development policies imposed on them'. MRG's work focuses on non-dominant ethnic, linguistic or religious communities who may not necessarily be in a numerical minority. These can include indigenous and tribal peoples as well as migrants and refugees. But such communities may not want to be classified as minorities, largely because the word 'minority' often has a negative connotation.

Official definitions

For official definitions of indigenous and tribal peoples, one must start by turning to the International Labour Organization's (ILO) Convention No 169 Concerning Indigenous and Tribal Peoples in Independent Countries (1989). This came into force in 1991, and replaced an earlier 1957 Convention. The ILO distinguishes indigenous from tribal peoples in the following way, saying the Convention applies to:

• Tribal peoples in independent countries whose social, cultural and economic conditions distinguish them from other sections of the national community and whose status is regulated wholly or partially by their own customs or traditions or by special laws or regulations;

• Peoples in independent countries who are regarded

as indigenous on account of their descent from the populations which inhabited the country, or a geographical region to which the country belongs, at the time of conquest or colonization or the establishment of present state boundaries and who, irrespective of their legal status, retain some or all of their own social, economic, cultural or political institutions.

• Self-identification as indigenous or tribal shall be regarded as a fundamental criterion for determining the groups to which the provisions of this Convention apply.[3]

This is one of at least three main working definitions within the United Nations (UN), which people refer to in the absence of anything else. Though it has a Draft Declaration on the Rights of Indigenous Peoples, the UN does not have an official definition of indigenous peoples, despite being urged to do so by indigenous leaders for more than ten years. The other two widely used definitions were suggested by UN rapporteurs Dr José R Martinéz Cobo and Mme Erica-Irene Daes, and are called after the names of their creators. In his 1986 Report for the UN Sub-Commission on the Prevention of Discrimination and Protection of Minorities, Dr Martinéz Cobo wrote:

'Indigenous communities, peoples and nations are those which, having a historical continuity with pre-invasion and pre-colonial societies that developed on their territories, consider themselves distinct from other sectors of the societies now prevailing in those territories, or parts of them. They form at present non-dominant sectors of society and are determined to preserve, develop and transmit to future generations their ancestral territories, and their ethnic identity, as the basis of their continued existence as peoples, in accordance with their own cultural patterns, social institutions and legal systems.'[4]

Erica-Irene Daes, Chairperson of the UN Working Group on Indigenous Populations, suggested this variation, designating certain peoples as indigenous:

• because they are descendants of groups which were in the territory of the country at the time when other groups of different cultures or ethnic origins arrived there;

• because of their isolation from other segments of the country's population they have preserved almost intact the customs and traditions of their ancestors which are similar to those characterized as indigenous; and

• because they are, even if only formally, placed under a State structure which incorporates national, social and cultural characteristics alien to theirs.[5]

Over at the World Bank, they have yet more definitions:

'The terms "indigenous peoples", "indigenous ethnic minorities", "tribal groups", and "scheduled tribes" describe social groups with a social and cultural identity distinct from the dominant society that makes them vulnerable to being disadvantaged in the development process. For the purposes of this directive, "indigenous peoples" is the term that will be used to refer to these groups... Because of the varied and changing contexts in which indigenous peoples are found, no single definition can capture their diversity. Indigenous peoples are commonly among the poorest segments of a population. They engage in economic activities that range from shifting agriculture in or near forests to wage labor or even small-scale market-oriented activities.'

This Operational Directive for World Bank staff goes on to say that indigenous peoples can be identified in particular areas by some or all of these characteristics:

• a close attachment to ancestral territories and to the natural resources there;

• self-identification and identification by others as members of a distinct cultural group;

• an indigenous language, often different from the national one;

• having customary social and political institutions;

• primarily subsistence producers.[6]

Why should the World Bank be concerned with such definitions? Because its staff need policy guidance to ensure that indigenous peoples benefit from development projects (too often, more powerful, non-indigenous groups get to the trough first). Also, to make sure they are not harmed by Bank-funded projects that affect their territories and communities. The Bank claims that it was the first multilateral financial institution to introduce a special policy towards indigenous and tribal peoples. It is worth remembering that these guidelines were only adopted after the Bank came under heavy international criticism for the devastating affects of mega-projects on indigenous communities in the 1960s and 1970s. It is currently in the process of revising this policy.

The gap between rhetoric and action

The major problem with the UN Draft Declaration (see later) and ILO Convention 169 is that the first is not yet adopted, and many countries have not signed up to the second. So all the definitions and conventions in the world do not yet help indigenous peoples to attain their rights. This is why the indigenous movement worldwide is calling for self-identification to be the main criterion for identifying indigenous peoples. However, some national governments reject the whole principle of self-identification. For example, the Indian Government has not signed or ratified Convention 169 and refuses to recognize the Adivasis or 'scheduled tribes' as indigenous. It claims that the whole population of India is indigenous. Other governments have said much the same thing. For example, when the UN declared 1993 the Year of Indigenous Peoples and various organizations asked the Botswana Government what this might mean for the country's San population, a minister retorted: 'All Batswana are indigenous'. It did not, therefore, see any need to make special arrangements for the minority San. The Government was also trying to emphasize the equality of all its peoples, and to defend the non-discriminatory principles of the constitution.

This opens up an interesting debate. In countries vulnerable to ethnic strife, whose governments may be working hard to achieve non-racialism and equality for all, is it justifiable to privilege one ethnic group over others, just because they claim indigenous status and demand special attention? On the other hand, given their vulnerability, marginalization and extreme oppression, it is recognized that indigenous peoples have particular collective as well as individual rights that afford them a specified level and quality of protection under international human rights law – just as women, children, refugees and certain other marginalized groups do. It is vital to stress that indigenous peoples demand recognition of their collective rights. The UN's Universal Declaration of Human Rights (1948) established the principle of universal rights for all, but emphasized individual rights. This resulted in states (where they abided by it at all) assigning rights to individual citizens, and sometimes dismissing the validity of collective rights based on cultural, ethnic or other forms of group identity. For example, in the Nordic countries the Sami's demand for collective rights is based on their status as one people. With the establishment of national Sami parliaments in Finland, Norway and Sweden, states that had previously favored individual rights finally recognized the principle of Sami group rights. This marked a major shift in attitude.

None of these issues is easy. People disagree constantly over terminology, never mind action or lack of it. Some scholars argue that the word indigenous should be dropped altogether, because it is – like the concept of tribes – 'essentialist', which means reducing people and things to universally fixed essences. When applied to people the theory of essentialism denies historical change and fluidity, the hallmark of human life itself.

Working definitions

Below is a summary of the main definitions.

• Indigenous peoples are non-dominant, non-state groups in a particular territory, who claim to be aboriginal (descended from the pre-colonial inhabitants). They identify themselves as indigenous and are regarded as such by others. They have distinct social, political and cultural identities, and languages, traditions, legal and political institutions that are distinct from those of the national society. They have a special relationship with the land and natural resources, which is often fundamental to their cultural identity and therefore their survival as distinct peoples. They are not industrialized, often subsistence producers, and they tend to be marginalized by wider society.

• Tribal peoples are much the same as indigenous, but they do not or cannot always claim to be descended from the original inhabitants of a territory. 'Tribal', like tribe, can be insulting, so the term is best avoided unless people choose to describe themselves this way.

• First Peoples, First Nations or First Nations people are those who claim to be descended from the original inhabitants of a territory.

• Minorities are people who are in the minority in the country where they live, but not necessarily numerically. They can be non-dominant for ethnic, linguistic or religious reasons. They can include indigenous peoples.

• The Fourth World was a term used by the World Council of Indigenous Peoples (the organization no longer exists) to distinguish the lifestyles of indigenous peoples from those of the so-called First World (highly industrialized nations), Second World (the former communist bloc) and the Third World (developing nations).

• A useful rule of thumb is to consider how people prefer to describe themselves.

• Indigenous peoples claim the right to define what is meant by indigenous, and to have other people recognize them as such.

This *Guide* uses generic regional names such as Aboriginal, though there are often many subgroups within each indigenous population. Largely for reasons of space, the book does not give all these different names. There is no universally agreed lexicon that covers every group, so it is best to ask people what name they prefer. In the US, for example, people tend to align themselves with particular nations, such as the Mohawk Nation, also known as Kanien Kaha:ka.

A guide to some preferred names:

Native Americans or First Nations	*not*	*Indians*
Aboriginal peoples, First Peoples, First Nations or First Nations people (nb First Nations excludes mixed-ancestry Métis, and Inuit. Indian is used in Canada to describe indigenous people who are not Inuit or Métis)	*not*	*Native Canadians*
Inuit	*not*	*Eskimo*
San	*not*	*Bushmen*
Mbuti, Efe, Lese, etc	*not*	*Pygmies*

Indigenous world

There are more than 7,000 indigenous societies around the world. Some put this figure much lower at nearer 5,000, because they do not list different subgroups, or because they exclude groups that do not fit the official working definitions of indigenous. Hard figures are difficult to come by because censuses are not reliable. Current estimates put the number of indigenous peoples worldwide at somewhere between 300 and 500 million people.[7]

Speaking out

Self-determination and legal recognition of the rights to own, manage and control their lands are key demands. These demands are a cornerstone of what it

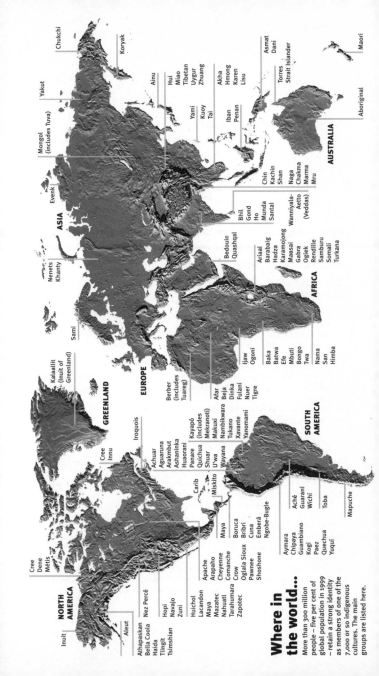

Where in the world...

More than 300 million people – five per cent of global population in 1999 – retain a strong identity as members of one of the 7,000 or so indigenous cultures. The main groups are listed here.

NORTH AMERICA

Cree
Dene
Métis

Athapaskan
Bella Coola
Haida
Tlingit
Tsimshian

Aleut

Inuit

Nez Percé

Hopi
Navajo
Zuni

Huichol
Lacandon
Maya
Mazatec
Nahuatl
Tarahumara
Zapotec

Apache
Arapaho
Cheyenne
Comanche
Crow
Oglala Sioux
Pawnee
Shoshone

Maya
Boruca
Bribri
Cuna
Emberá
Ngöbe-Buglé

Carib

Miskito

SOUTH AMERICA

Achuar
Aguaruna
Arakmbut
Ashaninka
Huaorani

Panare
Quichua
Shuar
U'wa
Wayana

Kayapó
(includes
Mekranoti)
Makuxi
Nambikwara
Tukano
Xavante
Yanomami

Aymara
Chipaya
Guambiano
Kogi
Paez
Quechua
Yuqui

Aché
Guaraní
Wichí

Toba

Mapuche

GREENLAND

Kalaallit
(Inuit of
Greenland)

Cree
Innu

Iroquois

EUROPE

Sami

AFRICA

Berber
(includes
Tuareg)

Afar
Beja
Dinka
Fulani
Tigre

Bedouin
Quashqal

Ijaw
Ogoni

Baka
Batwa
Efe
Mbuti
Bongo
Twa

Nama
San
Himba

Ariaal
Barabaig
Hadza
Karamojong
Maasai
Gabra
Ogiek
Rendille
Samburu
Somali
Turkana

Nuer

ASIA

Nenets
Khanty

Evenk

Mongol
(includes Tuva)

Yakut

Chukchi

Koryak

Ainu

Hui
Miao
Tibetan
Uygur
Zhuang

Yami
Kuoy
Tai

Akha
Hmong
Karen
Lisu

Iban
Penan

Bhil
Gond
Ho
Munda
Santal

Wanniyala-
Aetto
(Veddas)

Chin
Kachin
Shan

Naga
Chakma
Marma
Mru

Asmat
Dani

Torres
Strait Islander

AUSTRALIA

Aboriginal

Maori

means to be indigenous today. These and other claims are set out in the following example (see below), one of many declarations written by indigenous peoples for indigenous peoples.

United Nations' initiatives

The UN set up a Working Group on Indigenous Populations in 1982. One of its main tasks was to set standards, by drawing up a Draft Declaration on the Rights of Indigenous Peoples.

1995 marked the start of the UN's International Decade of the World's Indigenous Peoples (1995-

---

World Council of Indigenous Peoples' Declaration of Principles

'If we gather our voices into one... it will make us strong.'
Manesh, Innu elder, Canada.

1 All human rights of indigenous people must be respected. No form of discrimination against indigenous people shall be allowed.
2 All indigenous peoples have the right to self-determination. By virtue of this right they can freely determine their political, economic, social, religious and cultural development, in agreement with the principles stated in this declaration.
3 Every nation-state within which indigenous peoples live shall recognize the population, territory and institutions belonging to said peoples.
4 The culture of indigenous peoples are part of mankind's cultural patrimony [sic].
5 The customs and usages of the indigenous peoples must be respected by the nation-states and recognized as a legitimate source of rights.
6 Indigenous peoples have the right to determine which person(s) or group(s) is (are) included in its population.
7 All indigenous peoples have the right to determine the form, structure and jurisdiction of their own institutions.
8 The institutions of indigenous peoples, like those of a nation-state, must conform to internationally recognized human rights, both individual and collective.
9 Indigenous peoples, and their individual members, have the right to participate in the political life of the nation-state in which they are located.
10 Indigenous peoples have inalienable rights over their traditional lands and resources. All lands and resources that have been usurped, or taken away without the free and knowledgeable consent of Indian peoples, shall be restored to them.

2004). A milestone was reached in December 2000 when the UN created a Permanent Forum on Indigenous Issues. This spelled victory for indigenous peoples who had struggled for decades to win official recognition in the global community.

The 16-member Forum, which held its first session in May 2002, formally brings indigenous peoples and their representatives into the UN structure. For the first time, representatives of states and non-state groups enjoy equal status in a permanent representative body at the UN. Before, there was no permanent mechanism in the UN system to address the problems

11 The rights of the indigenous peoples to their lands includes: the soil, the subsoil, coastal economic zones all within the limits specified by international legislation.

12 All indigenous peoples have the right to freely use their natural wealth and resources in order to satisfy their needs, and in agreement with principles 10 and 11 above.

13 No action or process shall be implemented which directly and/or indirectly would result in the destruction of land, air, water, glaciers, animal life, environment or natural resources, without the free and well informed consent of the affected indigenous peoples.

14 Indigenous peoples will re-assume original rights over their material culture, including archeological zones, artifacts, designs and other artistic expressions.

15 All indigenous peoples have the right to be educated in their own language and to establish their own education institutions. Indian people's languages shall be respected by nation-states in all dealings between them on the basis of equality and non-discrimination.

16 All treaties reached through agreement between indigenous peoples and representatives of the nation-states will have total validity before national and international law.

17 Indigenous peoples have the right, by virtue of their traditions, to freely travel across international boundaries, to conduct traditional activities and maintain family links.

18 Indigenous peoples and their designated authorities have the right to be consulted and to authorize the implementation of technological and scientific research conducted within their territories and the right to be informed about the results of such activities.

19 The aforementioned principles constitute the minimal rights to which indigenous peoples are entitled and must be complemented by all nation-states. ∎

World Council of Indigenous Peoples' Declaration of Principles, ratified September 1984. The WCIP is no more. See www.cwis.org/fwdp/Resolutions/WCIP/wcip.txt

facing indigenous peoples. Though some are skeptical (see final chapter), most have high hopes that the Forum will make a real difference to improving their lives.

The big goal now is to get the universal declaration adopted. There are many ongoing arguments over the wording of the draft document. The stumbling blocks include whether or not some national governments will agree to the words 'peoples' or 'a people' to refer

UN Draft Declaration on the Rights of Indigenous Peoples

This includes the claims that indigenous peoples:

• have the right to the full and effective enjoyment of all human rights and fundamental freedoms recognized in the Charter of the United Nations, the Universal Declaration of Human Rights and international human rights law;

• are free and equal to all other human beings and peoples in dignity and rights, and have the right to be free from discrimination of any kind based on their indigenous origin or identity;

• have the right of self-determination, including the right to autonomy and self-government;

• have the right to participate fully in the political, economic, social and cultural life of the State while maintaining their distinct political, economic, social and cultural characteristics;

• have the collective right to live in peace and security as distinct peoples and to be protected against any type of genocide;

• have the collective and individual right to maintain and develop their distinct characteristics and identities, including the right to identify themselves as indigenous;

• shall not be forcibly removed from their lands or territories;

• have the right to practice their cultural traditions and religions, and use their own languages;

• have the right to recognition of their distinctive and profound relationship with their lands and territories; the collective and individual right to own, control and use these, and prevent interference or encroachment upon these rights; and the right to restitution of lands, territories and resources which have been confiscated, occupied, used or damaged without their free and informed consent. Where this is not possible, they have the right to compensation. ∎

Edited excerpts from the UN Draft Declaration on the Rights of Indigenous Peoples, viewable online through UN websites or at www.cwis.org

to indigenous peoples. There are disagreements over whether to use the terms 'territory' or 'land rights', and 'self-determination' as well as 'self-government'.

Ways of living

Indigenous peoples can be distinguished according to their different ways of life – how they survive and produce. These days, many have left their traditional life behind for the towns and cities, or work for wages part of the time and return to the land at other times of year. But the following descriptions still apply to hundreds of thousands of indigenous peoples worldwide, whether full- or part-time. People often practice mixed livelihoods; someone may be a pastoralist as well as a hunter-gatherer and cultivator, and earn cash in other ways too. But in most cases, the so-called subsistence economy is still the bedrock of how indigenous peoples make their living. These ways of living allow people to survive in very tough environments, wasting little or nothing, and are highly sustainable so long as there is enough space in which to move. That is changing as the industrial world encroaches upon indigenous peoples' fragile habitats.

Pastoralism

This pattern of life centers around animals, including cows, sheep, goats, reindeer, camels, yaks, horses, buffalo, llamas and alpacas. Pastoralists depend on the products of their livestock for food, clothing, implements, oil, shelter materials, barter and trade. Livestock are also a mobile form of wealth, medium of exchange and symbol of close relationships. They are used to pay bridewealth. Some people see their animals as sacred, certainly god-given. Many pastoralists are nomadic or semi-nomadic, moving seasonally between highland and lowland pastures in search of grass, water and salt-licks. They also move to escape ticks and tsetse flies that cause fatal stock diseases, or to get away from wild game such as wildebeest that

> 'As nomads we traveled constantly, never staying in one place for more than three or four weeks. This constant movement was driven by the need to care for our animals... seeking food and water to keep them alive.'
> *Waris Dirie, Somali, East Africa.*

infect cattle with a disease called malignant catarrhal fever. By moving seasonally, stock-keepers allow pastures to regenerate. Land, water and other resources in a particular area are shared communally. It is now widely recognized that pastoralism is a sustainable way of using certain types of fragile ecosystems, such as arid lands and difficult mountain areas.

Hunting and gathering

People hunt animals and birds for food, and by-products such as fur, skin and feathers that can be made into clothing and household goods. As well as hunting, fishing and trapping, they also collect edible insects, grubs, fungi and plants such as roots, fruits, berries and nuts. All these items can also be sold or bartered. Besides food, these resources also provide medicines, stimulants, pesticides, poisons, bedding and building materials. Fibers can be woven into baskets and mats. Forest-dwelling people also gather honey; many see this as the most prized food in the forest. People like the Inuit of Alaska and Greenland fish all year round, but hunt other animals seasonally: seals and nesting birds in the spring, other sea mammals such as walrus over the summer and caribou in the autumn.

Some hunter-gatherers, such as the 'Pygmy' peoples of Central Africa (best referred to by the name of their particular group), are called 'immediate return' societies. That means they focus on the present, people get an immediate return for their labor, and most food is consumed the same day as it is gathered. The opposite are 'delayed return' societies in which work is spread out over many months and there is no immediate yield. (Capitalist Western society is the ultimate example of this, but agricultural and pastoralist systems also broadly follow this pattern.) Hunting and gathering people usually live in non-hierarchical societies, which emphasize sharing and equality.

Subsistence agriculture

This includes peasant farmers and shifting cultivators, who often complement their agriculture with hunting, fishing and the collection of wild foods. Subsistence farmers cultivate on a small scale, often on tiny plots of land, and may produce enough to feed their families but have little or no surplus to sell. Increasingly, subsistence farmers are forced to earn a living as day laborers on commercial farms or as seasonal migrant workers. Examples of indigenous peasant farmers include the upland Quechua people of Ecuador and the Aymara of Bolivia.

Shifting cultivation, sometimes also called 'slash and burn', is a type of agriculture followed by indigenous peoples in the tropical regions of Central Asia and lowland South America. Whole villages may move often, relieving the pressure on a piece of land. For example, the Kayapo people in the Brazilian rainforests plant out gardens in forest clearings and also hunt, gather and fish. The range and number of crops they grow help to offset any failures. The Karen of Burma grow rice in a 7-year cycle. They clear trees, burn vegetation, plant and harvest, moving to a new site every year, before returning to the original site after seven. This allows the forest and thin soils to recover before they start planting again. Naga people in India and Burma also combine slash and burn with tilling more permanent irrigated rice terraces, making the most of their steep hilly terrain.

> 'Men do the sowing and women, singing choruses and working with tiny hoes in a line behind, cover the grain with earth. This system also provides an opportunity for romance.'
> *Nagas*, see www.angelfire.com/mo/Nagaland/culture.html

For reasons of space and practicality, this *Guide* does not cover every indigenous

> 'Every living animal that roams the country and every edible root that grows in the ground is common property.'
> *Yagan, an Australian Aboriginal man, in 1843.*

society in the world. For example, it does not say much about the Roma, partly because they do not appear to self-identify as indigenous, and are not recognized as indigenous by the UN (although they are seen as indigenous by the Center for World Indigenous Studies and there is an argument for including them).[8] But the book tries to give a broad overview, with as many representative examples as possible from different cultures, quoting indigenous people directly where possible. Many of the issues are contentious, so readers (including indigenous peoples) may not agree with everything.

The next chapter looks at what happened when explorers and colonizers first came across indigenous peoples. It was called 'discovery' – though of course, these people were there all the time. All 'discovery' meant was that Europeans found something and somebody new to them when they set sail to explore the outside world.

1 For more information, see Roxanne Dunbar Ortiz, *Indians of the Americas: Human rights and self-determination* (Zed Books 1984). **2** From www.iwgia.org **3** ILO Convention No 169, Article 1. Viewable at www.unhchr.ch/html/menu3/b/62.htm **4** '*Some Reflections on the Minority/ Indigenous People Dichotomy*', viewable at www.cwis.org/fsdp/internation-al/untrtst2.txt **5** From www.iwgia.org **6** Edited version of *Operational Directive on Indigenous Peoples, September 1991*, The World Bank Operational Manual, www.worldbank.org **7** This is the figure used by the Center for World Indigenous Studies (CWIS), who point out that there is no reliable aggregate number for indigenous peoples worldwide, hence it is safer to use the spread of 300 to 500 million. **8** UN recognition, and self-identification, will also tend to determine which other ethnic groups are included here.

2 Colonialism and conquest

First contacts with the outside world... explorers and colonizers... followed by missionaries, anthropologists and administrators whose policies were often oppressive... trail of disaster left behind.

ALTHOUGH PREJUDICE against and oppression of indigenous peoples is as old as the hills, the rot really set in with colonialism. When the European powers began carving up the world between them, they paid little regard to the local people who got in their way. In many cases they set out to exploit or exterminate them. Colonialism had a particularly devastating effect on indigenous peoples, because they were marginalized anyway, and had little or no power to resist. What follows applies to many communities, but to indigenous peoples in particular.

'The Indian must be made to feel he is in the grasp of a superior.'
Massachusetts clergyman George E Ellis, 1882.

'Kill every buffalo you can. Every buffalo is an Indian gone.'
Colonel RI Dodge, US Army, 1870.

'But our Young men seeing several very handsome Young girls they could not help feasting their Eyes with so agreeable a sight... the poor young Girls seemed a little afraid, but very soon after turned better acquainted.'
George Robertson, master of the Dolphin, Tahiti, 1766-68.

'The Masai [sic] are a decadent race who have survived through being brought under the protection of British rule... They remain primitive savages who have never evolved and... in all probability, never can evolve.'
Rupert Hemsted, Officer in Charge of the Maasai Reserve, Kenya, 1921.

'The inhabitants of New South Wales, both male and female, go without apparel... From a disagreeable practice they have of rubbing themselves with fish-oil, they smell so loathsome, that it is almost impossible to approach them without disgust.'
Mary Ann Parker, A Voyage Round the World, 1795.

New national boundaries were drawn up, which cut across ethnic lines and put false divisions between people of the same race and language group. New systems of government and foreign laws were imposed, though some colonizers preferred to rule through local chiefs in a system called indirect rule, which left some of these traditional structures virtually intact. Native rights to land were not usually recognized, and vast areas were snatched for white settlement in the belief that they were 'waste lands' or 'empty lands'. Resources like water, forests and minerals were also taken over by colonial authorities, the church, individual settlers, commercial companies and the state, leaving local people struggling to survive on the worst patches of land. The transfer of plant species from the empire to Europe began an ecological imperialism (involving the 'theft' and control of indigenous fauna and flora) that has continued to this day. 'Native' reserves were created, corralling people in a kind of human cage where it was easier to control and tax them. Pastoralists were forced into reserves that stopped them moving seasonally in search of grazing and water. Then they were blamed for overgrazing and overstocking; they could not win.

In some countries, such as the US, Canada and Australia, aggressive attempts were made to assimilate indigenous peoples into the dominant society. Children were forcibly taken from their parents and sent either to white foster homes and adoptive parents or government-run boarding schools. The aim was to wipe out their culture, and make them act like whites. Children were beaten for speaking their own language, forced to wear European clothes and taught that European culture was superior. The result was a lost generation that developed a distorted image of themselves, low self-esteem and a great sense of loss. Indigenous peoples are still living with the legacy of what has been called 'acculturation as a weapon of war'.

First contact

First contact often spelled death for indigenous and other local peoples, especially if they did not submit to the whites. Exploration began in earnest from the fifteenth century onwards, when explorers set sail from Europe in search of riches, the source of the Nile (something that had long fascinated travelers to Africa), new territories and discoveries of all kinds.

Robinson Crusoe, Daniel Defoe's 1791 novel, has been called 'a blueprint for the British colony: nature tamed, the undergrowth cleared or made productive; the natives either faithful, trained servants like Man Friday, or dead, mowed down by disciplined soldiers with guns'.[1] The same could be said of explorers and colonizers from other nations. Brutality, theft of land and enslavement were three common hallmarks of first contact, though there were individual exceptions of Europeans who sided with native peoples and appreciated their rich culture. Here is how the Pende people of the Congo saw the Portuguese, as told by Pende oral historian Mukonzo Kioko:

'Our fathers were living comfortably... They had cattle and crops; they had salt marshes and banana trees. Suddenly they saw a big boat rising out of the great ocean. This boat had wings all of white, sparkling like knives. White men came out of the water and spoke words that no one understood. Our ancestors took fright; they said these were *vumbi*, spirits returned from the dead. They pushed them back into the ocean with volleys of arrows. But the *vumbi* spat fire with a noise of thunder. Many men were killed... From that time to our days now, the whites have brought us nothing but wars and miseries.'[2]

In the US, the Spaniard adventurer De Soto made a habit of accepting the hospitality of friendly 'Indians' and then turning on them, killing and wounding people, kidnapping their leaders and burning crops and villages. His aim was to make indigenous peoples 'stand in terror of the Spaniards'. Fortunately for them he died in 1542, in what is now Arkansas. His henchmen, fearing that the locals might take revenge, ran away. Relationships between some immigrants and indigenous races were initially warmer than this. Christopher Columbus (Cristóbal Colón), arriving in the Caribbean in 1492, told his royal patrons, the king and queen of Spain, that the local Arawak people were wonderfully generous and handsome. He claimed part of the Caribbean for Spain, was greeted as a dignitary and ally by the Taíno people and went home full of enthusiasm. But he saw the Taíno as potential serfs, telling his queen: 'They are fit to be ordered about and made to work'. The following year Colón returned to the region and founded the Spanish colony of Isabela on the island of Hispaniola. Gold was found, and indigenous people were enslaved to work in mines and plantations on their own land. They tried to resist and were brutally put down; the Spanish vowed that 100 Taíno would die for every European killed. By 1500 there were few Taíno left: 3 million of them had succumbed to massacres, famine, disease and slavery.

European immigrants to the US who are celebrated as heroes by mainstream society today included Ulysses S Grant who murdered Apaches, Andrew Jackson who killed Creek, Seminole and Cherokee people, and Thomas Jefferson who ordered the massacre of Shawnee and Kickapoo. Colonel John Washington, whose grandson became the first US president, executed Susquehannock leaders in Maryland in 1675; though tried for murder, he was not convicted. There are countless other examples from the New World.

What was happening elsewhere? German explorer Dr Carl Peters was notorious for the way he shot his way through East Africa in the 1890s. He believed in using bullets to show Africans who was boss, writing unashamedly of how he treated the Maasai: 'I have found... that the one thing which would make an impression on these wild sons of the steppe was a bullet from the repeater or the double-barrelled rifle, and then only when employed in emphatic relation to their own bodies.'[3]

When Captain Cook landed in Australia in 1770, he had been ordered by the Crown not to take land without native consent, or unless it was uninhabited, but he went ahead and claimed the east coast in the king's name. When the first boat came ashore, Aboriginal people attacked the visitors with spears, and were driven back by bullets. The British did not settle until 1788, when they claimed Aboriginal land, saying it was empty and belonged to no one. But Aboriginal people had been there for 60,000 years, living in 600 to 700 clans, each with its own territory, political system and laws. The earliest settlers were convicts, many of them transported for petty crimes and anti-government politics. They were later joined by 'free' settlers, come to make their fortunes in the new colony. The convicts, their jailers and the free settlers may have been very different types of people. But the majority had one thing in common: scorn for Aboriginal people, which often manifested in horribly cruel acts including rape and murder.

The scientist Charles Darwin (1809-82) came across Aboriginal people in New South Wales in 1836. He could see at once what their fate was:

'The number of aborigines is rapidly decreasing... wherever the European has trod, death seems to pursue the aboriginal. We may look to the wide extent of the Americas, Polynesia, The Cape of Good Hope and Australia, and find the same result... The varieties of man seem to act on each other in the same way as different species of animals – the stronger always extirpates the weaker. It was melancholy at New Zealand to hear the fine energetic natives saying that they knew the land was doomed to pass from their children.'[4]

Here he sounds sympathetic towards indigenous peoples. But Darwin's theories of evolution and natural selection were to have a massively harmful effect on relations between the so-called 'advanced' and aboriginal societies. The latter were said to be at a lower level of evolution, with smaller brains and less brainpower, and the unscrupulous and racists used this to justify slavery, apartheid, the Holocaust and colonial massacres. However, Darwin also wrote that the different races of humankind were descended from a common ancestor, and that there were many points of similarity between them.

Was first contact all bad?

In some places, there were limited benefits from first contact and first settlement. These included trade and employment, and some people happily intermarried, too. For a trade example, the captains and crews of early 16th century French and English fishing vessels, working off Canada's Atlantic coast, traded furs with indigenous peoples. Later, beaver pelts were much in demand for hat making in Europe, and again it was the local inhabitants who supplied them. Champlain, who founded the first permanent white settlement in Canada at Quebec in 1608, traded with Algonkians and Hurons, hired them as guides, and gave them military help in fighting their enemies, the Iroquois. But the poisoned chalice was guns: Indians soon found that they were far superior to their own weapons, and bartered their valuable products for arms. They lost the art of making their own weapons, fought among themselves for monopoly of the fur trade, and became more desperate as over-hunting decimated the animals they had relied upon. Over time, their social system broke down as they moved from hunting for their own use in migratory bands to hunting for trade, which could be done more effectively in family groups.[5]

Making people sick

Colonialism also brought new diseases, which struck down indigenous peoples in their thousands. The killers included measles, influenza, smallpox, typhus, whooping cough, TB and venereal diseases, to which local people had no immunity. Some colonizers deliberately killed indigenous people by giving them smallpox-infected blankets – stories are still told about this today in Canada and the US. An unidentified disease, very probably spread from white settlements, killed off all the Native Americans on a long stretch of New England coast in the 1600s. On signing a treaty with the newcomers in 1621, Massasoit, chief of the Wampangoags, told them: 'Englishmen, take that land, for none is left to occupy it. The Great Spirit... has swept its people from the face of the earth.'

The Spanish *conquistadores* under Cortés were able to subdue the peoples of Mexico in 1520 when smallpox (which had probably arrived on one of their ships) took hold, killing tens of thousands. Famine followed, after unharvested crops were left rotting in the fields. The conquerors and their later apologists saw these diseases as divine retribution for 'savage' sins. One 17th century author wrote about how Mexicans had been wiped out by 'vices, drunkenness, earthquakes, illnesses and recurring epidemics of smallpox and other diseases with which God in His mysterious wisdom has seen fit to reduce their numbers'. The silent killer then traveled to South America overland through the Maya kingdoms of Central America, across Panama and over the Andes. It is said to have wiped out half the Incas, including the emperor Huayna Capac and his eldest son and heir.

Venereal disease was allegedly introduced to Australia by Europeans, though the settlers called it 'black pox' and blamed Aboriginal people for infecting them. Settlers frequently shot dead Aboriginal women they suspected of having given them the pox. Decadent sailors took the disease across the oceans; months at sea, when they were unable to get proper treatment, made their state all the worse by the time they arrived on land, desperate for sex with the nearest available women. Tahitians claim that explorer

Louis De Bougainville's sailors first brought venereal disease to their island paradise in 1768.

All told, whether deliberate or accidental, some estimates put the numbers of people who died as a result of newly introduced diseases at 80 to 90 per cent of the original populations in North America, large parts of Central and South America, Australia and Aotearoa/New Zealand.

Here are some examples of population slumps from disease and other factors linked to colonialism: Australian Aboriginals fell from at least one million pre-colonially to 30,000 by the 1930s; Maori from a quarter million to 42,000 by 1890; Polynesians on Tahiti from 40,000 in 1769 to 6,000 by the 1840s; 11 million indigenous Americans died in the 80 years after the Spanish invaded Mexico; Indians in Brazil fell from at least 2.5 million to 225,000 after Portuguese conquest (recent archeological evidence suggests that the pre-conquest population figure is probably much too low); more than 8 million Incas lost their lives in the Andes; the numbers of Native Americans north of Mexico fell from more than 8 million to 800,000 by the end of the 19th century. At least 11 million Africans were sent as slaves to the Americas, but millions more are believed to have died en route. Many were left to die before they embarked, or died as a result of activities linked to slavery.[6] In the Congo, Central Africa, the population was cut by at least half between 1880 and 1920.[7] Smallpox and sleeping sickness were spread by the mass population movements that came with colonialism. One European visitor described seeing a 15-foot boa constrictor feasting on the flesh of smallpox victims, and vultures so full they could not fly.

Working for Europeans could be the end of you, too. Slavery was obviously the most extreme example, but other types of labor were also forced. This book does not examine pre-20th century slavery, because it is difficult to separate the victims who were indigenous from those who were not. The Portuguese were exposed by the pioneering British journalist Henry Nevinson for running slave plantations on the islands of Saõ Tomé and Príncipe off West Africa with what they called 'indentured laborers' shipped from the mainland, years after the abolition of slavery. These may well have included members of African communities who identify themselves as indigenous today. In 1915 the death rate on the islands was estimated at 100 per 1,000 laborers. Before roads and railways, human porters were used to transport goods all over Africa, and they died in their thousands from disease, malnutrition and overwork, not to mention being eaten by lions.

A little later, even when people supposedly gave their labor willingly, new taxes forced Africans (and people in other parts of the empire) into wage labor in order to raise the necessary cash. They were recruited and conscripted into armies and police forces, hired to build public works like roads and railways, and press-ganged into working on plantations where conditions were terrible. All this movement was fatal for many laborers. Workers often had to travel far from home, to unfamiliar climates where they died of cold or fever. Many more Africans succumbed to disease and malnutrition, after being forcibly conscripted into Kenya's Carriers Corps in World War One, than those who died in combat – a staggering one in four of all conscripts died. (The Carriers Corps supplied porters for British soldiers fighting the Germans in East Africa. A suburb of Kenya's capital city, Nairobi, is still called Kariokor today.)

The killing fields
Probably the very worst abuses in colonial Africa took place in King Leopold's Congo. Up to ten million Africans, indigenous and otherwise, are said to have died in the course of the Belgian monarch's bid to rape central Africa for rubber and other riches, from 1885 onwards. The Welsh explorer and journalist

Henry Morton Stanley (he claimed to be American, one of his many lies) had paved the way for Leopold some years before, by staking claims to the Congo on his behalf. Stanley – wrongly hailed as a great hero, then and since – also did his share of killing Africans and burning villages. One member of his party stuck the severed head of an African in a box of salt and sent it to London to be stuffed and mounted by a taxidermist.[8] Under Leopold, the suffering continued on a massive scale. This was state-sponsored terror. People had their hands cut off for failing to supply enough rubber, and hands and feet were also cut off corpses to prove to officials how many Africans had been killed in a given area. Others were flogged or jailed for disobedience, while women and children were taken hostage until their villages had provided the set quota of rubber. Starvation struck villages which had lost their productive adults, or because they were forced to supply Leopold's soldiers with vegetables and fruit.

Some colonizers deliberately massacred indigenous peoples to get them out of the way, or by engineering tribal wars, encouraged one group to fight another and do their job for them. This is how the Governor of Louisiana congratulated himself on triggering a war between the Choctaw and

Last of the Tasmanians

One of the last Tasmanian Aboriginal people was Truganini, daughter of a chief. She saw her mother stabbed to death by whites, her sister kidnapped and her uncle shot dead. Aged 15, she and her fiancé were taken by a couple of white men on a boat ride. The sailors threw her partner overboard. He could not swim and clung desperately to the boat. The white men chopped his hands off; after he drowned, they raped Truganini.

She later came to live on Flinders Island, where the last community of Tasmanian Aboriginals was confined. Even in death, she suffered humiliation. According to Aboriginal custom, she should have been cremated. Instead, her skeleton was put on show in Hobart Museum. In 1976, Truganini's remains were at last cremated and her ashes scattered in the sea. ∎

Chickasaw peoples in the 17th century:

'The Choctaws... have raised about 400 scalps and make 100 prisoners... [This] is a most important advantage that we have obtained, the more so, that it has not cost one drop of French blood, through the care I took of opposing these barbarians to one another. Their self-destruction in this manner is the sole efficacious way of insuring tranquillity in the colony.'[9]

In Tasmania, most of the Aboriginal inhabitants were either murdered or died of introduced disease between 1804 and 1834, and the remnants were put on an island in the Bass Strait between Tasmania and Australia where they literally pined away. The so-called laws of natural selection were used (here and elsewhere) to justify such murder as a duty. Rape was also commonly used as a weapon and demonstration of white male control. Stockmen on Tasmanian farms regularly kidnapped Aboriginal women for sexual purposes. One of the most notorious episodes took place in 1827 at Cape Grim, when some white shepherds tried to take advantage of the local women. Their menfolk intervened, there was a fight and two people were wounded, one on each side. In revenge the Aboriginal men attacked the shepherds' flocks, and killed 118 sheep by spearing or throwing them over the cliffs. The shepherds had the last word. They killed at least 30 Aboriginals, throwing their bodies after the sheep.[10]

In some African colonies, soldiers were sent on so-called 'punitive expeditions' to suppress tribal revolts. In German East Africa the Germans hanged twelve Barabaig elders and their chief medicine man, Gidamowsa, leaving their bodies to rot on the scaffold as a warning to others. Often the warriors of one group were hired to attack their neighbors, and were 'paid' in loot such as raided cattle. Pastoralists who had lost thousands of stock in the rinderpest epidemics at the end of the 19th century were only too happy to help because they recouped their losses in this way. But some African populations slumped between 1880 and 1900 as a result of these raids and the starvation that followed them because farming was disrupted.

German colonizers brutally suppressed the Maji Maji rebellion in German East Africa in 1905-7 – the most serious challenge by Africans to colonial rule in this period. They also massacred Herero people in German South West Africa (now Namibia) between 1901 and 1906. The Herero revolted in 1904, killing 100 Germans, destroying some farms and raiding cattle. The response was far more vicious: between 75 and 80 per cent of the total Herero population of 60,000-80,000 were killed, women and girls were raped before being bayoneted, 14,000 people ended up in prison camps and 2,000 fled to South Africa. Soon after the Herero rose up, so did their neighbors the Nama. The Germans seized their land and livestock, so the Nama had no way of surviving. They were offered food and jobs if they gave themselves up. After their leaders Jacob Morenga – hailed as a kind of African Robin Hood – and Hendrik Witbooi were killed in battle, the Nama lost the will to fight on.

Bibles and labels

In the footsteps of the explorers came missionaries and later anthropologists. There is a much-repeated saying about how indigenous peoples lost their land, which crops up in different parts of the world with slightly different wording: 'With one hand you gave us the Bible, and with the other you took away our land'. In other words, we were distracted and duped. That is not quite true in every case – missionaries were by no means all bad, and they did not always have the power to take the land, though colonial rulers and governments did. On the positive side, missions offered education to non-whites at a time when the state did not. Education became the route out of oppression and poverty for many, and former mission pupils helped to liberate their countries from colonialism in the independence struggles of the 1950s and 1960s. Some early missionaries were quite radical and opposed government oppression of 'native' people. But most missionaries tended to scorn local customs, lifestyles, dress, language, religion and spirituality. Their main aim was 'improvement', on the assumption that indigenous and tribal peoples were at a low stage

Live human exhibits

In the age of high imperialism, from about 1850 to 1915, it became fashionable to put 'primitive' people on show at exhibitions. It was the age of Great Exhibitions, or World's Fairs as they were called in the US, and people flocked in their millions to see human freak shows presented as 'educational'. Photos of colonized peoples also became very popular, mostly taken by anthropologists and travelers. Many of these images, and the whole tone of such exhibitions, were racist. Their main message was that indigenous people were more primitive and backward than Europeans.

They did not just hurt the individuals who took part, physically and emotionally. They also helped to justify colonialism, and damaged the communities these people came from, many years after the event. They peddled ideas about racial difference and 'savagery' that are still current today. 'Bushmen' (San) were placed alongside baboons. Supposedly historical re-enactments of events like the Matabele War of 1893 showed Africans being defeated by white heroes. Non-whites, particularly women, were shown naked and eroticized to feed Western fantasies. At the US exhibitions, Native Americans were often shown in the most negative light.

Circus showman Phineas T Barnum was behind many of these displays, which masqueraded as seriously anthropological. Barnum's Ethnological Congress in 1880 featured a human parade made up of misshapen, non-white bodies ('ugly' people, and so-called dwarfs and giants) contrasted with those of 'perfect' white Americans. Barnum liked to describe his exhibits as savage cannibals who spoke no English. In fact, his three 'Fijian man-eaters' shown at the Philadelphia Exhibition in 1876 had been brought up on a Christian mission, were not cannibals, and spoke good English.

Ota Benga, a Mbuti 'Pygmy' from the Congo, was taken to the US as an object of curiosity. He appeared in the St Louis World's Fair of 1904, the New Orleans Mardi Gras and even at the Bronx Zoo. Later he lived in an orphans' home in Brooklyn, and attended a seminary in Virginia. Unable to take any more humiliation, he committed suicide in 1916. ∎

of human development. They railed against polygamy and tried to stamp it out, ignoring the fact that a man's 'spare' wives and children would be effectively thrown on the scrap heap and left to fend for themselves. They tried to force nomads to settle in one place, where they could be preached at more easily. They forced people into trousers, skirts and shoes. They tried to stop people speaking their own tongue, forcing children into schools where the main 'diet' – taught in a Western language – was religious dogma. (Later, the curriculum broadened to include more useful subjects; if lucky, you got a missionary who took a real interest in the advancement of his or her pupils.)

The earliest, self-styled anthropologists were often colonial administrators who studied local customs and languages as a hobby. They set about classifying the races of the new colonies. People were pigeon-holed according to how 'savage' they seemed, on a sliding scale from civilized to savage human being. Darwinism and the theory of natural selection were popular new ideas, and influenced how non-Western people were categorized. These classifications have stuck to people ever since – in Africa and other parts of the world today, some non-indigenous people still look down on indigenous peoples as a lower form of life.

Prejudice against nomads and hunter-gatherers

In the colonial period many indigenous peoples were classified 'savage' and 'primitive' because they were not cultivators but pastoralists or hunter-gatherers. The idea that people who till the soil are more civilized than others is an ancient one, linked to the idea that settled people can make permanent improvements in their lives, both physical and intellectual.

Prejudice against nomads is very deep-seated. People who wander about have been dismissed for centuries as aimless, uncivilized, uncontrolled and therefore a threat to the state, greedy for more land than they actually need or use. In a 1937 study of nomads, anthropologist Ragnar Numelin wrote: 'The more primitive [man] is, the greater is his geographical influence and it then decreases to the degree in which he succeeds in becoming its master. In higher stages, the wandering need becomes materially modified'.[11] He called the cattle-keeping nomads of North Africa 'an army of loafers'. Nomads in general were 'cultureless peoples' with a 'psychological problem bound up in the wandering instinct'. It was a short step to saying nomads had small brains, and sure enough, he did.

Comparing the Maori favorably with other indigenous peoples who did not cultivate, the Archbishop of Dublin said they 'were very far from being in as low a state as the New Hollanders [Australian Aboriginals], for they cultivated the ground, raising crops of the *cumera* (a sweet potato), and clothed themselves, not with skins, but with mats woven by themselves'.[12] Lord John Russell, British Secretary of State for War and the Colonies from 1839-1841, also said approvingly that Maori people were 'not mere wanderers over an extended surface... in search of a precarious subsistence'.[13]

These ideas are very persistent. Roma and travelers have been dismissed for similar reasons, and equated with vagabonds and thieves. Hunter-gatherers do little better, often being described scornfully as backward forest people who must 'develop' if they want to be accepted by mainstream society. Today, whether indigenous peoples are still living in the old ways or not – keeping livestock or hunting and gathering, living in the city and working in an office – former prejudices remain. Old labels stick to new bottles, keeping indigenous peoples sidelined and 'justifying' bad treatment by governments, organizations and individuals.

The noble savage

There is a flip side to the coin that denounces indigenous peoples as savages, which is to exoticize them as 'noble savages'. This is just as bad in the end, because it still means that they and their rights are not taken seriously. They can end up like beautiful beasts in a human zoo, on display for everyone to stare at and photograph. Indigenous peoples who live in or near national parks and game reserves complain that this is how some tourists treat them – as an extension of the wilderness. The concept of wilderness is itself deeply problematic and ethnocentric.

The idea of the noble savage came from French philosopher Rousseau, writing in the 18th century. He believed that humans, in their original state, were beautiful, glorious and carefree; they only became corrupted and tainted by civilization. When the first travelers reached Tahiti (Wallis in 1767, Bougainville in 1768 and Cook in 1769), they saw it as an earthly paradise. European readers fell upon their journals in delight, believing that they confirmed Rousseau's ideas about the noble savage. The writer Diderot, a friend of Rousseau's, reacted differently. When he read Bougainville's account of the Tahitians, he urged that they should be left alone. Addressing the Tahitians, he wrote: 'One day they [the Christians] will come, with crucifix in one hand and the dagger in the other to cut your throats or to force you to accept their customs and opinions; one day under their rule you will be almost as unhappy as they are.'

And the story goes on...

What colonialism and first contact began, the modern world has continued to do. At independence, power was handed over to local élites who pushed a nationalist agenda that was often unsympathetic to indigenous peoples. In many countries, these élites have hung on to power ever since, ruthlessly suppressing dissent. Giant industries, hydroelectric dams and mining operations have displaced thousands of indigenous peoples from their land. Their knowledge is 'ripped off' in the name of scientific advancement. Many are still seen as 'uncivilized', and the non-indigenous world looks down on them with contempt. The next chapter examines the problems facing indigenous peoples today, many of which stem directly from colonization and the attitudes it spawned, for imperialist attitudes helped to shape long-term policies towards indigenous peoples.

1 Felix Padel, 'Forest knowledge: tribal people, their environment and the structure of power', in RH Grove, V Damodaran, S Sangwan (eds) *Nature and the Orient*, (Oxford University Press 1998). 2 Adam Hochschild, *King Leopold's Ghost*, (Papermac 2000). 3 Carl Peters, *New Light on Dark Africa*, (Ward, Lock & Co 1891). 4 Charles Darwin, *Journal of Researches into the Natural History and Geology of the Countries visited during the Voyage of HMS Beagle Round the World* (no publisher given 1839). 5 Adapted from *Canada's Indians*, MRG Report No 21 (1982). 6 Mark Cocker, *Rivers of Blood, Rivers of Gold: Europe's conflict with tribal peoples* (Pimlico 1999). 7 Hochschild, *Ghost*, quoting Jan Vansina. 8 Hochschild, *Ghost*. 9 From James Wilson, *The Original Americans: US Indians*, MRG Report (1986 edition). 10 Cocker, *Rivers of Blood*. 11 Ragnar Numelin, *The Wandering Spirit* (Macmillan 1937). 12 R Whately, *On the Origin of Civilisation* (London 1855). Cumera is kumara. 13 Russell to Hobson, 9 December 1840, CO 380/122, Public Records Office, London.

3 Land and nature

Land and the natural world... rights and claims... knowledge, spirituality and creation myths... women and nature... urbanization... and the dangers of romanticism...

LAND IS LIFE ITSELF for many indigenous peoples. Their lives revolve around land and natural resources such as pasture, forest, honey, water, salt-licks, wildlife, domestic animals and wild plants that provide food and medicine. Unlike the majority of non-indigenous folk, they do not tend to see the natural world in terms of profit – it has deeper meaning, other kinds of value. However, that is changing as greed, cash and Western values such as individualism reach into every corner of the globe. What follows refers to many, but not all, indigenous peoples.

The natural environment is at the heart of their identity and culture. The human life cycle mirrors that of the natural world, and is believed to be circular rather than linear. One of the best examples of this is Australian Aboriginal beliefs about the Dreamtime. Aboriginal people relate totally to the earth, derive their spiritual power from it, and draw from the Dreamtime their ideas about how best to look after the environment. They believe the spirit of life exists for ever, and manifests itself in the landscape.

Knowledge of the environment
People who live largely by pastoralism, hunting, gathering or fishing have to know their environment intimately – they can almost read it like a book. They even come to know it as a kind of person with shifting moods; the relationship is a highly personal and emotional one. They must learn to manage the environment sensibly and sustainably or risk losing the bedrock of their lives and ecosystems.

Living on the land for generations, indigenous

In the Dreamtime

Aboriginal people call the process of creating the world the Dreamtime, or in North Queensland, the Storytime. They believe that the world was created by many male and female ancestors in the form of birds, animals, fish, insects, clouds, thunder, water, and also items made by people, like spears and *dilly* (string) bags. These beings came out of the earth, and made all the features of the landscape. Along the way, they often changed from human to animal, bird to plant, and other transformations. When they had done what they came to do, they went to ground again. There they stayed for evermore, in particular places, becoming a source of spiritual power. They are linked by stories or 'songlines' and nurtured by people acting out – through ritual and in their everyday activities – what the beings did in the Dreamtime. These actions mirror the myths and keep them alive. The landscape is believed to be animated by these beings. People often say their ancestral land is their mother or father, who has 'brought them up' and nourished them. Though the landscape is both male and female, women play a big part in the Aboriginal belief system. 'Spirit children' are believed to jump up into women's wombs at water sources or sacred sites, and this spirit presence is revealed through a sign appearing in the landscape. This may take the form of a bird or animal behaving in an unusual way, or appearing in an unexpected place. Such a place is believed to be the child's spiritual home, and he or she is considered responsible for that piece of land.

Every aspect of life is explored in the ancestral myths, and all the stories are very practical – they tell people how and where to hunt, gather food, cook, store things and make tools. Therefore myths combine practical knowledge with spiritual knowledge. When they die, people believe they return 'home' to be reunited with their totemic being, such as a bird, fish or wallaby. They must go back to a specific place; no other place will do.

'We come back la our own country again… when I die they gonna send my spirit back here, that's my home see, my land. I gotta come back here. We bin come from here, we gotta come back here. Same place.'* ■

*Quote from an interview with Winston Gilbert, by Veronica Strang in Alaine Low and Soraya Tremayne, *Women as Sacred Custodians of the Earth? Women, spirituality and the environment* (Berghahn Books 2001).

peoples come to know where and when to find honey, nutritious or medicinal wild plants, track down animals to kill and eat, find the best grazing, water sources and salt-licks, or catch the biggest fish. They know how to find and stitch certain leaves together to

> 'The white man made us many promises, more than I can remember, but they never kept but one; they promised to take our land, and they took it.'
> *Red Cloud, Lakota leader, North America, 19th century.*

make cups, plates and other household goods. They know that the twigs of some trees make excellent toothbrushes, certain leaves make natural deodorants, and the boiled bark of other trees is good for the digestion. A certain kind of grass makes good bedding, because the smell keeps biting bugs away. One herb cures coughs, another diarrhea. Tea made from a particular root cures fever. And if you want to get 'high', or mask the pain of illness or injury, there is always something natural you can take. Often such people live in very harsh environments, where anyone else would soon starve or die of illness, far from any modern hospital.

For example, by following the wisdom and traditions of their ancestors, the San people[1] of southern Africa were able to survive in very dry areas by gathering nutritious wild plants and by burying water in ostrich shells along the routes they traveled. Today, their lifestyle is changing as they have lost their land to game reserves and cattle herding, which has taken over large areas of their traditional territory. But those who still hunt use poisoned arrows – with poison made from natural substances – and cleverly track their prey for many miles until the wounded animal becomes drugged and falls down. They use every part of the animals they hunt, taking care not to hurt females and their young. To take the example of just one San group, the Ju | 'hoansi or !Kung (found in Namibia, Angola and Botswana) live off 55 different species of animal, eat more than 100 different species of wild plants and know exactly where to collect vegetables and fruits that ripen at different times of year.[2]

The Sanema people of Venezuela live in the rainforest. They move their farm plots often, practicing a low-impact form of agriculture that allows the soil to recover. The types of crops they plant – bananas, cassava, plantains and yams – take the minimum from the nitrogen-poor soil. They supplement their diet with meat and other forest produce, going into the forest to live temporarily and hunt with bows and arrows. The Tukano people of Brazil and Colombia practice sustainable fishing, striking a fine balance between their food needs, the needs of the fish and the wellbeing of the forest, too. The Tukano fish only certain areas of the Uaupes River; each community decides what part of river they will fish, leaving some stretches alone, which allows them to become spawning grounds. Cultivation and the felling of trees along river banks is banned, because it is believed that these areas belong to the fish.

As Paulinho Paiakan, leader of the Kayapo people of Brazil, puts it: the rainforest is 'our university'.

Traditional environmental knowledge (TEK)

Traditional environmental knowledge now has a label – TEK. Some people also call it ethno-ecology. Western scientists increasingly recognise its value; they want to learn from it, and document it properly. Indigenous peoples are demanding the right to take part in this kind of study on their own terms. They are wary of having their knowledge stolen by Western drug companies, who have made a lot of money out of indigenous medicine. Many of the prescription medicines derived from plants, and now available globally, were only discovered through talking to indigenous peoples.

Now some indigenous groups are taking steps to patent plants, so that they can retain a measure of control over their scientific and medical uses. One current example is a joint initiative by a Maori scientist, Dr Meto Leach, and elders of the Tuhoe, a Maori tribal group. But other Maori (and other indigenous groups elsewhere) are not agreed that such attempts to patent plants are useful for protecting the traditional knowledge base. It is a controversial area.

The Traditional Environmental Knowledge Pilot

Project of the Dene Cultural Institute of Canada is one example of recent TEK research, done in collaboration with the Dene people of the Northwest Territories. In 1989, Dene researchers joined forces with a biologist and an anthropologist to document Dene environmental knowledge. The aim was to integrate Dene TEK and Western science, and develop a community-based natural resource management system. The study has covered such subjects as animal ecology, habitats, feeding habits, the relationships between different species, life histories, migrations, population cycles and how animals respond to changes in their environment.

In common with many other indigenous peoples, the Dene believe in taking care of the land and its resources for future generations. That includes hunters avoiding certain areas for a time, to allow the number of animals to increase, and only hunting mature animals, not

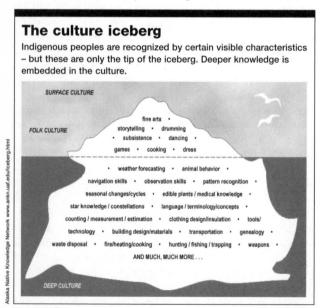

The culture iceberg

Indigenous peoples are recognized by certain visible characteristics – but these are only the tip of the iceberg. Deeper knowledge is embedded in the culture.

SURFACE CULTURE

FOLK CULTURE

fine arts •
storytelling • drumming
• subsistence • dancing •
games • cooking • dress

• weather forecasting • animal behavior •
navigation skills • observation skills • pattern recognition •
seasonal changes/cycles • edible plants / medical knowledge •
star knowledge / constellations • language / terminology/concepts •
counting / measurement / estimation • clothing design/insulation • tools/
technology • building design/materials • transportation • genealogy •
waste disposal • fire/heating/cooking • hunting / fishing / trapping • weapons •
AND MUCH, MUCH MORE . . .

DEEP CULTURE

Alaska Native Knowledge Network www.ankn.uaf.edu/iceberg.html

pregnant females or those caring for young.[3]

Another good example of collaboration using TEK between scientists and indigenous peoples took place recently in Aotearoa/New Zealand. The Ngati koi people (a tribal group, or *iwi* in Maori) worked with researchers from the National Institute of Water and Atmospheric Research (NIWA) on the history of the Ohinemuri River, North Island. Together, they presented historical evidence of ecological damage, largely caused by gold-mining, in their claim to the Waitangi Tribunal, which is hearing Maori claims arising from the colonial Waitangi Treaty made between Maori chiefs and Britain. Science and traditional knowledge came together to record this history. Besides looking at old archives, the team also gathered oral evidence from Maori people. 'Our people have more than 80 years' experience of the river,' says Ngati koi spokesperson Joel Williams. 'They also have the recollections of their ancestors, who have resided along the river for over 12 generations.' The river used to be home to thriving quantities of whitebait, eel and fish, while the forest around it used to teem with birds. The biodiversity of the river is now much reduced.[4]

Bryce Cooper of NIWA explains what the Ngati koi were trying to prove: 'Their traditional uses of the river and its margins (for example, eels as a food source, flax for weaving) have been damaged by the activities of the European settlers – gold-mining, farming, sewage discharges. Also, in Maori tradition the status of an *iwi* or tribal group is built upon the good quality of the natural resources over which it has stewardship rights.'[5] The research concluded that the river and its surroundings had indeed been severely damaged. The scientists could not have proved this on their own, says Bryce Cooper. 'Ngati koi knowledge added much to the case as it provided a longer time scale of information than was possible from our science data, and supported our science inferences regarding the past character of the river and what fish populations could have been there prior to farming and gold-mining.' The Waitangi Tribunal is still considering the evidence.

Collective ownership

The idea that land can be privately owned is usually anathema to indigenous peoples. They see it – and other resources like water, plants and wild animals – as something belonging to the whole community. You have to share it. You do not grab more than your fair share. You do not plunder everything in sight without putting something back. And you cannot buy and sell it, as Crowfoot, a Blackfoot Native American chief, tried to explain to white Americans:

'Our land is more valuable than your money. It will last forever... As long as the sun shines and the waters flow, this land will be here to give life to men and animals. We cannot sell the lives of men and animals. It was put here for us by the Great Spirit and we cannot sell it because it does not belong to us. You can count your money and burn it within the nod of a buffalo's head, but only the Great Spirit can count the grains of sand and the blades of grass on the plains. As a present to you, we will give you anything we have that you can take with you; but the land, never.'[6]

The South American Incas made sure that everyone had access to land which was held by the *ayllu* – the community or kinship group. In the Western Ghats area of south India, tribal peoples used a form of shifting cultivation called *kumri* that allowed them to manage communally-held land in an ecologically sound way. (The colonial British saw the cultivators as barbaric vagrants, and banned *kumri* because they said it threatened the forests.)[7] The whole basis of Native American society was co-operative, and that included the way people managed their environment. In colonial Africa, European powers took advantage of the fact that most ethnic groups did not 'own' land in the Western sense, and seized millions of acres – calling it 'vacant' and 'wasteland'. But from the African savannas to the Australian outback and the North American plains, tribal and indigenous peoples saw land and the natural world as something to be shared. These attitudes began to change with colonialism. After Europeans began arriving and staking claims to land, some indigenous leaders realized that although they had legitimate customary rights to their lands, they had better stake a European-style legal claim, too, or see it all disappear. Hence some went to court or registered land titles in an attempt to defend what was theirs in the first place. To this day, indigenous peoples are demanding recognition of their ownership of traditional lands, not simply their rights to use and occupy it.

Spirit realms

Land and nature are not seen as separate from the rest of life. The spiritual, the social and the material are all entwined, and everything is believed to connect with everything else. That makes indigenous people literally feel more grounded than people who have lost their roots, often in the concrete jungle.

The environment is a sacred realm. God or gods are not generally believed to take a human form, as they do in say Christianity or Hinduism, but inhabit the natural world itself. God is thought to be all around, living in the landscape, and the earth is revered like a parent. Native Americans, for example, believe in a cosmic unity that embraces human beings, animals, plants and everything else. Humans must live in harmony with the whole or suffer the consequences. Shamans mediate between people and spirit beings in the landscape by performing various rituals, but ordinary people must also show respect for the spirits by obeying strict rules about hunting, eating and other activities. Before whites arrived and the economy began to change, the very existence of the Inuit people of Canada, Greenland and Alaska depended on being able to interpret the environment. They also believed it was inhabited by spirits, both good and bad, who could be influenced through shamans (see chapter 6).

Siberian reindeer herders, the Evén people, believe you must not whistle, sing or make a noise when out in the wilds because this might offend the spirits who own the forest. To be a successful hunter you must also respect the moods of animals and behave in a quiet, unobtrusive way. It is all about showing respect – even if you kill something. Damara herders of Namibia also believe one must stay silent when gathering wild foods out of respect for the ancestors, whose help is needed to collect them. They also guarantee people's safe passage through ancestral land. The Naga people of Asia believe both in a supreme god – a creator who is rather remote – and in earth spirits which have different functions. One is believed to be the goddess of crops and wealth, another the one who presides over all wild animals, and so on.

> 'Land is my backbone. I only stand straight, happy and proud and unashamed of my color because I still have land.'
> *Aboriginal man, Australia.*

According to the Maori creation story, in the beginning was Te Kore or total darkness. There was no life, just potential. The Earth Mother, Papatuanuku, and the Sky Father, Ranginui, were locked in an embrace that shut out all light and prevented anything growing. Their children desperately wanted light, so they separated their parents by force. One of the sons, Tane Mahuta or God of the Forests, got between earth and sky. He pushed up as hard as he could with his legs until his father was prised apart from the earth. The God of the Winds, God of the Sea and all living things poured into the light that was created. Tane Mahuta made the first human being from the clay of his mother. He slept with her and made a daughter, Hinetitama. With Hinetitama, Tane conceived other children. When Hinetitama found out that her father and lover were the same person, she ran away to the underworld, where she still lives.

Earth mothers: women and the natural world

Some people see women as the sacred custodians of the earth. Why? They give birth to new life, tend the earth and harvest its fruits, protect and nurture, and often play a central part in rituals to do with fertility, making rain, blessing earth, animals and crops. Spirit mediums are often women, who communicate between the spirit world, the environment and human beings. But some anthropologists and feminists argue that bracketing women with 'nature' brackets men with 'culture' and therefore places men in a more powerful and superior position – because culture is associated with reason and civilization, nature with something lower and wilder.

Either way, rural indigenous women tend to live very close to the natural world. Before hospitals arrived, and even afterwards, the women's task was to find and gather medicinal plants and cure the sick. Women and children collect the wild foods that form an important part of the diet. They make clothing and other items out of natural materials, both for use at home and to sell or barter. They teach children about the environment and spiritual values.

Chiefs used princesses to perform 'eco-rituals' in old Zimbabwe. One of them, Muredzwa, was so famous as a rainmaker in the 19th century that rain was said to fall into her footsteps as she walked by. This ancient institution of princesses, whose jobs included enforcing 'traditional ecological laws', has recently been revived. They have tried to stop sacred groves being cut down, told men off for fencing pools

'Everyone takes responsibility for what's going on, in the land and with the animals – not only the game officers... So there is great social pressure when these rules are not followed because our survival depends on the land and animals.'

Bella T'seleie of Canada's Dene people.[3]

that the whole community should be able to use, and banned the sale of caterpillars and locusts which they think god gave people to eat, not to sell.[8] At the same time, in Zimbabwe and other parts of the world, certain women have long been seen as a negative and dangerous force environmentally. An age-old fear in many cultures is that female witches blight crops, stop the rains coming and make animals fall sick.

Once were warriors

Urbanized indigenous people also retain a special link to the land. Though thousands of indigenous people no longer live in the countryside but in towns and cities, they are a significant part of the story. Most still feel deeply about the land, although they no longer live close to it. Some urban groups are now spearheading calls for indigenous land rights; they may be better placed than rural people to take on governments,

Wild foods: an example from southern Sudan

Nuer and Dinka people of southern Sudan eat wild foods as part of their everyday diet. Seeds, berries, leaves and roots help people survive when other food runs short, or famine looms. They are also eaten on ceremonial occasions; wild grass grains are traditionally given to the most important wedding guests. Wild foods are very nutritious, sometimes more so than introduced vegetables and fruits, and particularly important for children. For example, an average-sized Balanites tree will yield enough nuts to feed a family of six for one month in terms of calories alone. Poor women can sell wild foods to keep the family going – you will see wild foods for sale in local markets. Some fruits even find their way north to Khartoum, the capital, where they are eaten dried or as cakes. The Dinka use 149 different foods made from wild plants. Some are named after birds or animals – such as *abuth gook*, or dove's pumpkin, and *joljong*, meaning dog's tail. Others have places named after them, or describe how the food tastes – such as *cuei*, meaning sour.

Yet the image we have of war-torn southern Sudan is of starving people dependent on Western grain dropped from planes. Though aid saves some people's lives, trying to end famine by dumping grain (often surplus grain that Western countries do not want) can have the opposite effect. Local people may become dependent on an outside source corporations and lawyers. But this can lead to rivalry and jealousy, as more educated urban people speak on behalf of the silent majority. Some accuse urbanized people of getting an unfair slice of the cake, and doing this for personal glory, because they are closer to the seat of power – and may even be powerful politicians themselves. Conversely, urban people (and those of mixed ancestry) may have difficulty proving their rural roots and hence their territorial and other rights under treaties. In Aotearoa/New Zealand, there is an ongoing dispute over recognition of urban Maori groups. Treaty of Waitangi settlements have resulted in many tribal groups becoming powerful corporate players, but urban Maori have little or no claim to these *iwis* and are arguably missing out. In a continuing wrangle with the Government and among different clans over customary rights to sea fisheries, pan-tribal urban groups are demanding the right to fishing

---

of food, and famine only sets in when families leave their homes, land and livestock to rush to where the food aid is. Research shows that failing to value wild foods and recognize their importance in people's diets is very damaging. It shows no respect for natural resources and indigenous peoples' ways of coping. The causes of food insecurity and famine in southern Sudan are political, and food has long been used as a weapon by the main aggressor here – the Government of Sudan, which is fighting rebel forces in the south. Some elements in these southern rebel groups have also used food as a lever.

Journalists and aid agencies predicted in 1985, when famine struck again, that millions of Nuer and Dinka people would die unless massive amounts of food relief were sent in. But the numbers who actually died were far fewer. A critical review of aid efforts in southern Sudan concluded: 'The reason for the survival of such large numbers of people was their own food and economic resources, notably the reliance on wild foods such as berries and grasses during the critical months.' ■

Food and Power in Sudan: A critique of humanitarianism (African Rights, May 1997). The wild foods research was done by Caroline Gullick, 'Blessing or Burden? The importance of indigenous wild food plants in food security in southern Sudan with a focus on their significance to women and children', unpublished MSc thesis (University of Salford 1998).

> 'The surest way to kill us is to separate us from the Earth.'
> *Hayden Burgess, World Council of Indigenous Peoples.*

quotas despite not being able to lay claim to a stretch of coastline or membership of a specific band.[9]

Back on the land, things are also changing. Privatization has increased, and with it monetization – many traditional resources and goods have a price now, preferably in cash. More and more people are embracing Western-style individualism. Exploitation of land and resources by transnationals is not only 'raping' those resources but also changing local people's values and way of life, as the next chapter will describe. Now that people realize the worth of land title, land in certain regions is being chopped up into smaller privately-owned parcels, which are often too small to yield much. It has to be said that richer individuals, some of them indigenous, are themselves exploiting other indigenous people in this race to claim and carve up land. In some places, traditional ideas about sharing resources communally are being lost.

But beware too much romanticism...

Reverence for nature should not be confused with ecological soundness in all cases. Aboriginal peoples were not necessarily the world's first ecologists, as some people claim. Western awe of non-Western societies that live 'close to nature' can obscure the fact that some indigenous peoples' practices are not necessarily ecologically sound or sustainable. Or if they are, that came as a result of trial and error over many centuries. This awe can say more about Westerners themselves, disgusted by environmental destruction in their own backyard, looking eagerly to other societies to find something 'pure' and unspoiled. There is a need to be wary of blind reverence. It links to a long tradition in Western thought, which saw pre-colonial societies as living in harmony and balance with nature – always 'living lightly upon the land', almost childlike in their ways. That is patronizing and too simplistic. Indigenous peoples were and are just as capable as anyone else of manipulating the natural world to suit themselves, and there is evidence, for example, of fauna and flora disappearing over time as a result of over-hunting and over-burning of vegetation.

Control over land is power in its purest and most basic form because it involves control over food, and therefore the means of survival. What is the fate of indigenous peoples who have lost their land, forests and other natural resources? One old man, a Batwa 'Pygmy' from the Great Lakes region of Central Africa, put it bluntly: 'Since we were expelled from our lands, death is following us. We bury people nearly every day. We are heading towards extinction.'[10] The next chapter will explore these crises and related problems in more detail.

> 'We want our land. We can't plant rice in the heavens.'
> *Cambodian villager.*

1 The San do not have one name to describe themselves collectively. They are made up of 13 or more groups. But they prefer to be called San rather than the other names they have been given, such as Bushmen. They live in Botswana, Namibia, Angola, South Africa, Zimbabwe and Zambia. **2** Megan Biesele and Kxao Royal/O/oo, *San* (Rosen Publishing Group 1997). **3** Martha Johnson, 'Documenting traditional environmental knowledge: the Dene, Canada', in Hugo Slim and Paul Thompson, *Listening for a Change: Oral testimony and development* (Panos 1993). **4** *Aniwaniwa* online, Issue 17, www.niwa.cri.nz/pubs/an/17/science.htm **5** Personal communication, April 2002. **6** Miller, *From the Heart*. 19th century, no exact date given. However, this kind of statement has been exploited by governments who use it to claim that indigenous peoples had no traditional concept of land ownership prior to colonial contact. **7** Subash Chandran, 'Shifting Cultivation, Sacred Groves and Conflicts in Colonial Forest Policy in the Western Ghats' in Grove, Damodaran, Sangwan (eds) *Nature*. **8** From Terence Ranger, 'Priestesses and environment in Zimbabwe' in Low and Tremayne, *Women as Sacred Custodians*. **9** Information from *IWGIA, The Indigenous World 2000-2001* (IWGIA 2001), p189. **10** Unnamed man from Kalehe, DRC, quoted in Jerome Lewis, *The Batwa Pygmies of the Great Lakes Region*, MRG Report (2000).

4 Facing the problems

Looking at problems today, with an historical dimension... Examples from around the world highlight land losses and encroachment by mining, logging, oil companies and large-scale commercial farming... the impact of tourism... refugee crises and conflict... slavery... loss of language... and disease.

LOSS IS THE WORD that links many of the problems facing indigenous peoples today. Land loss is the most crucial, for without land there is no viable life and livelihood. Given the links between environment and identity, discussed in the last chapter, land loss also undermines cultural identity and wellbeing in a very fundamental way, and this explains why the land rights issue is central to almost every declaration by indigenous peoples. After being torn from their lands, other losses are never far behind including loss of resources, customary foods and plant medicines, extended family, language, freedom to roam, and the freedom to practice their own customs and religious rites in a place of their choosing. Forced urbanization has brought countless problems. For all these reasons, some indigenous peoples are on the brink of extinction.

Indigenous peoples are among the most disadvantaged and discriminated against human beings in the world. They are often the poorest, with the worst health, housing, schooling and job opportunities. They suffer high rates of depression and other mental health problems, suicide and substance abuse. Sometimes they are denied access to health services, welfare and schooling altogether. Where state schooling is offered, it may be used by governments as a tool for assimilation – in a bid to replace indigenous languages and culture with dominant, national ones.

In some cultures, indigenous women are in a subordinate position and enjoy few rights, though the

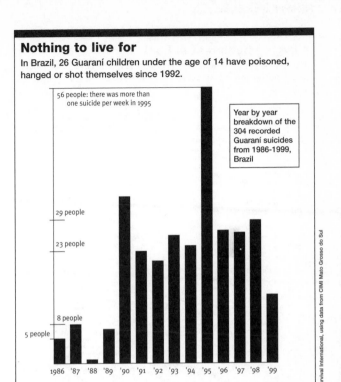

Nothing to live for

In Brazil, 26 Guaraní children under the age of 14 have poisoned, hanged or shot themselves since 1992.

56 people: there was more than one suicide per week in 1995

Year by year breakdown of the 304 recorded Guaraní suicides from 1986-1999, Brazil

29 people

23 people

8 people

5 people

1986 '87 '88 '89 '90 '91 '92 '93 '94 '95 '96 '97 '98 '99

Survival International, using data from CIMI Mato Grosso do Sul

bigger threat usually comes from national society. They are vulnerable to rape and sexual exploitation, especially by soldiers, police, employers and other powerful males. There have been shocking exposés of the high rates of black deaths in custody (such as those in Australia since 1980) – the result of police brutality, but passed off as suicide and 'misadventure' – and murders by police and the military in places like Colombia. Many of the victims are indigenous community leaders, targeted purely because of their efforts to achieve land and other collective rights (see chapter 5). It is also no accident that many 'down and outs', living on city streets in wealthy countries such as Canada, the US and Australia, have

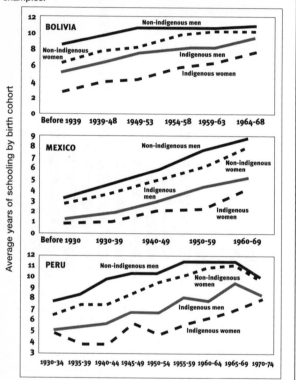

Lagging behind at school

Indigenous peoples, both male and female, lag far behind the rest of the population in their access to education. Below are three examples.

indigenous ancestry. Despairing and destitute, they have dropped off the map of the rich world.

Exploitation of land

Many of the indigenous peoples who survived into the 20th century did so because they lived in areas that once had no value for others. But companies now roam the globe looking for new resources to exploit.

States, also driven by the profit motive, are eager to exploit resources they once saw as marginal and uneconomic. Expanding populations, the discovery of minerals and oil, the growth of modern communications and other factors have now ended the isolation of even the most remote indigenous groups. Indigenous lands are threatened by agriculture, roads, dams, irrigation projects, mines, oil extraction and timber logging. There are also many cases of pastoralists being evicted from their grazing lands to make way for wildlife parks. These are suddenly declared 'conservation areas' in which humans are said to have no place – which ignores the fact that pastoralists have often happily coexisted with wildlife for centuries, and helped to conserve and shape the very environment that is so prized by Western-dominated 'conservation' bodies. The same is true of hunter-gatherers and most shifting cultivators, too.

These activities are often linked to national development projects that ignore the welfare of indigenous peoples. Their resources are being taken without compensation. When they resist, they feel the full force of state repression. They are blamed for being backward, for not embracing modernity. But why should they embrace 'development' that has been designed by and for others? Below are some stories to illustrate the point.

Example 1: the Barabaig, Tanzania, East Africa

'This was prime grazing land. We can ill afford to lose such a large area of pasture.'[1]

Barabaig pastoralists lost a vast area of their most productive pastures to a Canadian aid-funded wheat scheme from 1970 onwards. Their government did not stop this; on the contrary, it signed up to the Tanzania Canada Wheat Program and handed over 100,000 acres to the National Agriculture and Food Corporation, to grow wheat by Canadian prairie-style mechanized methods. The wheat farms took over more than 12 per cent of Hanang District, where the Barabaig live, but the loss was much more than the size of land involved. It encroached upon a type of pasture they call *muhajega*, made up of nine very important species of grass and herbs. After the wheat farms came, and through other types of encroachment, the Barabaig lost virtually all their *muhajega*. They have been forced to over-rely on other kinds of pasture. Grazing that was once rested seasonally has been used more intensively, pastures are deteriorating and the herds do not produce as much as they did. Other environmental impacts include soil loss, bush clearance and gully erosion.

But there have been some positive outcomes. The Barabaig people launched an international campaign to defend their rights, and a legal challenge. A High Court judge ruled that they did have communal rights to the land, and that the wheat growers had trespassed, but no land was actually returned to them. In 1994 the Tanzanian Government appointed a Commission on Violations of Human Rights in the wheat farming areas. Its report was not made public, but it apparently confirmed the truth of Barabaig claims.[2]

Example 2: the Yanomami, Brazil

'This is what we want – to live in peace. We are tired of death, of murders, of the destruction of the forest.' *Davi Yanomami*

Yanomani are rainforest people, living deep in the Amazon near the border with Venezuela. They had little contact with the outside world before the 1980s, when a gold rush prompted thousands of miners to invade their territory. This exposed them to killer diseases to which they were not immune, and to violence from miners and other settlers. One fifth of Yanomani were killed by disease and violence in just seven years during the 1990s. The roar of supply planes and the constant noise of generators and pumps used in mining scared away many of the game animals they hunted. High-pressure hoses have washed away river banks, silting up the rivers and destroying spawning grounds. Mercury, used to separate gold from soil and rock, has been dumped in the rivers and poisoned people's food and water. The influx of miners has caused social upheaval that has led to a rash of begging, prostitution and drunkenness.

The Yanomami campaigned, with support from Brazilian and international lobbyists, for their lands to be declared a reserve. This was seen to be the best way of safeguarding their culture and future. The Brazilian Government finally created a special territory in 1992.

More land losses

● wealthy ranchers have taken lands belonging to the Awá in Brazil and the Enxet in Paraguay, while commercial oil palm plantations threaten Awá and Chachi forest territories in Ecuador.

● uranium mining and nuclear testing have destroyed Aboriginal lands in Australia.

● a World Bank-funded road virtually wiped out Nambiquara people in Brazil.

● Gana and Gwi (San) people in the Kalahari have seen their houses razed, families trucked to bleak resettlement camps and water supplies cut off in a long-running attempt by Botswana's government to drive them off their lands.

● Bagyéli 'Pgymy' peoples in Cameroon have lost access to natural resources as a result of a World-Bank funded pipeline cutting across their lands.

● copper and gold mining has wrecked indigenous lands in West Papua (Irian Jaya).

● logging has decimated forests used by Dayaks in Malaysia.

● Adivasi communities in India have been forced off their lands in the Nagarhole National Park to make way for an 'eco-development' project.

● oil and gas drilling companies, and loggers, have threatened to drive the Khanty and Udege people of Siberia off their lands.

● loggers and settlers have invaded and desertified the lands of the Wichí people of Argentina.

● lands belonging to Mapuche communities in Chile have been fragmented and taken over by industrial forestry plantations.

● the Innu of Labrador and eastern Quebec have lost land to mining concessions. ■

From Survival International's reports; other information supplied by Tom Griffiths.

Cleaning up polluted land

Expenditure on clean-up of contamination on 800 First Nation reserves in Canada (2001). Most pollution comes from hydrocarbon seepage into the soil from storage facilities. The rest is from waste, asbestos, and air and water pollution.

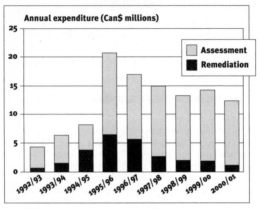

www.ainc-inac.gc.ca

Since then the Yanomami have set up their own health, education and bee-keeping projects, which have improved their situation. But this has not stopped the invasions. There was a massacre of 16 Yanomami by miners at Haximu in 1993. The latest threat comes from the Brazilian army, which wants to build more barracks in Yanomami lands. The military presence has again led to disease, and the sexual exploitation of women. Miners have also returned. The Yanomami still urgently need full recognition of their land ownership rights, to protect them from further incursions.[3]

Conflict

Indigenous peoples are right in the firing line in conflicts around the world. In some cases, that is because their leaders have defied oppressive national governments and stood up for people's rights to self-determination. Indigenous peoples often happen to live in buffer zones between different nations and power groups who are at war. Sometimes they live in areas with rich resources coveted by transnational corporations, and war is being fought over rights to these resources.

Example 3: the Karamojong, Uganda

The Karamojong pastoralists of north-eastern Uganda are a long way from Washington. But the 'New World Order' is impacting on them in surprising ways, as the post-September 11 anti-terrorism campaign leads to repressive measures against African pastoralists who need guns to ward off cattle raiders, just as many US citizens carry them for self-defense.

Clare Short, British minister for international development, has said that 'collapsing states, where people live in poverty and misery, provide opportunities for international terrorists to organize and hide themselves'. The 'warriors against terrorism' are now keen to support 'failing' states against any group of people who prefer to regulate themselves and who reject mainstream values. The 'New World Order' simply does not tolerate diversity. There is evidence that Washington is behind current Ugandan Government efforts to disarm the Karamojong forcibly, as if they threaten to destabilize the 'civilized world'. This ignores the historical and cultural facts about this Nilotic people, who number more than a third of a million and comprise the Dodoso, Jie and Karimojong [sic].

When cultural resistance involves modern firearms, a small ethnic group can easily be seen as a threat to world security. There was a flood of weapons into this area after Idi Amin's troops fled the local barracks in 1979, leaving a full arsenal of AK-47s. The idea is that, by removing the guns, this corner of Uganda will return to normal, and world leaders will sleep more soundly in their beds – for one more state will have been saved from failing. But there is no evidence that any international terrorists are being harbored here, or that the Karamojong are a threat to anyone besides their immediate neighbors.

Now the state is showing that it is also a raider, by confiscating thousands of livestock, often for the personal gain of army officers. Soldiers have repeatedly committed atrocities – beating, torturing, looting, raping, shelling villages and killing. All the Karamojong want is to be left alone (although their neighbors might complain about government inaction). Their elders pray that outsiders will stop interfering in their affairs. In April 2002 elders performed a ritual curse against such people by throwing gravel behind them through their knees, to the west.

There is a sense of déjà vu here. The colonial British, who first saw the Karamojong as a 'law and order' problem, are still remembered for their initial brutality. Said one Jiot man: 'People were tied to trees and shot or nailed through the head... The British had guns, so we did not confront them. Their rolling volleys were too much for us.' Then and now, guns may affect the technological balance of power. But the state, holding a monopoly on guns, does not stop them being used against certain people.[4]

Example 4: the Montagnards of Vietnam

The 53 indigenous ethnic minorities of Vietnam have had a long history of struggle with central government, from French colonialists to the communist state. They have suffered land losses and also been 'used' by both sides in conflicts, including the Vietnam War, when US Special Forces organized ethnic minority highlanders known collectively as Montagnards (from the French term 'mountain dwellers') into defense groups to prevent communist infiltration from the north. Though the rights of ethnic minorities are now enshrined in the Vietnamese constitution, their situation remains uneasy. Politicized highlanders today increasingly refer to themselves as Dega. Below, a man from Dak Lak, interviewed in July 2001,[5] tells the story of the struggle...

'Since god gave birth to the world, we ethnic minorities have always been in the same place. Since antiquity, our

ancestors have always told us that this is our land. The Vietnamese never lived here. What we learned from our grandparents is that Vietnam started invading our land in 1930... From the time the French left in 1954, the Vietnamese increased their presence until they were all over the place. In 1958, because the Vietnamese were getting stronger and stronger in the Central Highlands, all the ethnic minorities – Ede, Koho, Jarai, Stieng and Bahnar – stood up to make the first demonstration. All the ethnic minorities had one idea: we wanted our land back. The Vietnamese promised to give us our land back so there would be no more conflicts. They were not speaking the truth. Instead, they put our leader, Y Bham Enuol, in jail in Hue for seven years.

In 1965 when they let Y Bham out of jail, the ethnic minorities started the FULRO movement. It was based in Cambodia. I was 12 years old and carried a gun that was as long as me. Everyone, young and old, joined the struggle. Later, in 1969, Nguyen Van Thieu, the president of South Vietnam, promised in the '033' agreement to give us our land back. Y Bham would be in charge of the Central Highlands and the Vietnamese would go back to Vietnam. Instead, Vietnam received foreign aid and used the Dega to fight against North Vietnam. Thousands of us were killed. In 1975, the [North] Vietnamese put our leader Nay Luett in prison for ten years. Vietnamese from both the north and the south took Dega labor to plant rubber and coffee. When the harvest came, they sent it to the lowlands. They used all sorts of tricks to destroy the ethnic minorities and take our land. Many Dega went to prison.

Beginning in 1980 they started turning all the land over to the Vietnamese. Each day more and more Vietnamese arrived, by the truckload... We [FULRO] conducted a struggle in the forest to oppose them for many years. The life of Vietnamese and Montagnards together is like dogs biting each other; never easy.'

Refugee crises

People are often made refugees as a result of conflict. Such crises can also be triggered by 'natural' disasters such as floods and drought, and other human-made catastrophes such as ethnic cleansing and genocide. Again, indigenous peoples are highly vulnerable to becoming refugees and internally displaced persons – those forced to move within their own countries rather than across borders. Indigenous and tribal refugee populations include the 160,000 or more Saharawi people from Western Sahara who have to live in refugee camps in Algeria because Morocco illegally occupied their lands. There are also Kurds, scattered around the world; Afghan tribal peoples, seeking refuge everywhere from Australia to Britain; Roma (Gypsies), fleeing persecution across Europe; the Muslim Rohingya people of Burma (Myanmar) who have fled to Bangladesh, while the Karen, Mon and other groups have gone to Thailand. The Nagas live in a state they call Nagalim, or Nagaland, on the junction between China, India and Burma; some of them have become refugees. Chakma people of the contested Chittagong Hill Tracts, Bangladesh, have sought refuge in India and Burma in their thousands. At least 50,000 Chakma were also displaced by the Kaptai Dam reservoir.

Tourism

Tourists have taken over where the early explorers left off – seeking leisure, pleasure and excitement in remote parts of the world. Now there are millions of them, and unwittingly or otherwise, they may trespass on indigenous people's territory and do other kinds of damage along the way. Unless run by and for indigenous communities on their own terms, so-called 'eco-tourism' is not any better, because it brings tourists into closer contact with indigenous peoples through 'tribal encounters'.

Sue Wheat of Tourism Concern explains the difficulties facing an organization campaigning for ethical and fairly traded tourism.

'The other day we got a phone call from a TV production company. They were making a program about "badly behaved

tourists" and wanted some stories. I explained that we did not point the finger at tourists but looked more at how the tourism industry affected local people and environments.

I told her about one of the cases we were researching for an article in our members' magazine, *In Focus*: 250 Filipino villagers' homes had been demolished, 17 people wounded and four people seriously injured in evictions from a lake area designated for "eco-tourism".

The researcher was aghast. "But I thought eco-tourism was about protecting environments," she said. "Yes. But it doesn't always work well for people," I pointed out. I told her about the San people who have been harassed and tortured to force them off their land. One tactic was to tie people who remained in the Central Kalahari reserve to wildlife rangers' jeeps and drag them through the bush. And about Maasai in Tanzania, who are again facing eviction from the Ngorongoro area because of conservation, and about fishing villages in Brazil that face eviction because of big tourism resorts.

Eviction of people is one of the most serious impacts of tourism on indigenous peoples. But they also often find that tourism revenue by-passes them as so much tourism is controlled by outsiders. Their images are used to market a place, but they are rarely consulted about whether they want tourism. And they pay severe social and environmental costs when tourist numbers increase beyond a level that they can sustain. Those that do set up their own community-based tourism businesses often find it difficult to market themselves to tourists in Europe and the US from their remote communities.

Although shocked and concerned, like so many researchers who have come before her, the TV researcher could not use the information. "It's too worthy," she said. "But I'm sure someone else will take it up."

The problem is that so few people do. 2002 was designated by the UN as the International Year of Eco-tourism, and a World Summit on Eco-tourism was held in May in Canada. The summit was full of environmentalists, tour operators and tourism officials, and a smattering of indigenous people who managed to get funding to attend. Big operators were not present, which indicates the interest from the mainstream tourism *industry. A Declaration on Eco-tourism was written to be taken to the World Summit on Sustainable Development. It proved quite a struggle for indigenous representatives to change the declaration from a largely promotional one, to something that also reflected indigenous views and concerns about tourism.*

There are of course, a lot of communities that want and rely on tourism. Communities in Ecuador, for instance, are using eco-tourism as a means of preventing oil prospectors from taking over their land, and communities in the Philippines are benefiting enormously from the economic advantages brought by bird watchers to their island. Increasingly, indigenous peoples are realizing that tourism could be a vital economic lifeline for them – but only if they are able to control it and benefit from it. We are working with groups worldwide to make sure this can happen.'[6]

Negative portrayal

Derisory and negative descriptions of indigenous peoples crop up everywhere. In even 'quality' journalism,

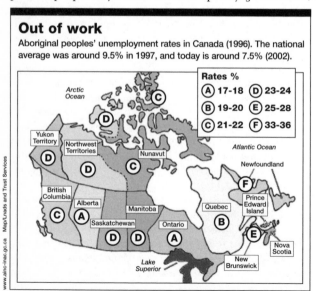

Out of work

Aboriginal peoples' unemployment rates in Canada (1996). The national average was around 9.5% in 1997, and today is around 7.5% (2002).

Rates %
(A) 17-18 (D) 23-24
(B) 19-20 (E) 25-28
(C) 21-22 (F) 33-36

Arctic Ocean

Atlantic Ocean

Yukon Territory (D)

Northwest Territories (D)

Nunavut (C)

(C)

(D)

Newfoundland

(F)

British Columbia (C)

Alberta (A)

Saskatchewan (D) (D)

Manitoba (D)

Ontario (A)

Quebec (B)

Prince Edward Island

(E)

Nova Scotia

New Brunswick

Lake Superior

the indigenous person is the butt of every writer's joke, in ways that racism against say black or Irish people would no longer be tolerated.

One example from recent travel journalism was written by Lynn Barber of the UK's *Observer* newspaper, who visited the Inca city of Machu Picchu, Peru. The introduction describes how she 'joins a shaman as he invokes the god of fire with the help of a cigarette lighter'. Her account is full of gratuitous insults. She finds the shaman in the ruins at night: 'He was warmly and prosaically dressed in anorak and combat trousers – he looked like someone who would be helpful in B&Q [a chain of British home maintenance superstores]. But he had an exotic array of props on the carpet in front of him – two crystal skulls and a child's nightlight shaped like a serpent... Oomba, woomba, shoomba, he droned, while one of the acolytes explained that he was invoking the god of fire.' The writer describes, with barely concealed scorn, how the shaman raced around them waving condor feathers and banging a drum. She calls it 'being whooshed at'. What is going on here? The 'clever', 'knowing' Western writer has set herself at a distance from the object – the stupid, unknowing Indian who dresses like a British worker but behaves like a 'savage'. This is 'entertainment' produced at someone else's expense.[7]

Countless films have used indigenous people as extras, brought in to add 'exoticism' and a dash of 'savagery', accompanied by war whoops and drumming. The following story tells how a famous movie-maker got it wrong.

Example: a film-maker in Peru

In 1979 the German film-maker Werner Herzog arrived in Peru to make a film about Fizcarraldo, the rubber baron. He had reckoned without opposition from local Aguaruna Indians. The Aguaruna Council told Herzog he could not film in indigenous territory.

They did not want to take part in a piece of myth-making, in which a notoriously bloodthirsty person was portrayed as a considerate and eccentric music-lover obsessed with the idea of bringing opera to the Amazon. Herzog and his crew were sent packing from the area. This sparked a national debate in Congress that polarized opinion. The Aguarana won the day, persuading people that men who had built their fortunes on slavery, murder and oppression of indigenous peoples should not be allowed to represent Peru. Herzog was forced to shoot the film a thousand miles south in Ashaninka territory. Apparently, the Ashaninka did not have the know-how or political awareness to oppose him, and the film was completed with their assistance.[8]

Slavery

Modern slavery includes human trafficking, bonded and forced labor, domestic, sexual and other forms of slavery that should have been stamped out more than a century ago. Poverty, inequality and discrimination are at the root of this. Since indigenous peoples are often the poorest and least powerful of groups, they are vulnerable to being enslaved.

Example 1: forced labor and other abuses in Burma

Burma's military government has viciously cracked down on the pro-democracy movement in recent years. Anyone who opposes the state is liable to face counter-insurgency operations, forced labor and relocation, the destruction of homes and crops, extra-judicial executions and other gross human rights abuses. The best-known opposition figure is movement leader Aung San Suu Kyi. But also among the victims (and the resisters) are the Karen people and other indigenous groups. About a third of the country's population consists of ethnically distinct hill peoples. There are eleven main indigenous groups of whom the largest are the

Karen, Kachin, Shan, Chin, Palaung and Naga. The Karen struggle for independence is one of the longest-running indigenous rebellions in Asia.

Tens of thousands of indigenous people have been moved out of their villages at gunpoint to relocation sites where they are forced to labor for up to 15 days a month. They are forced to build public works and infrastructure such as roads, maintain army camps and porter for army patrols. At these sites, curfews and other bans control people's free movement and free speech. Soldiers openly loot their belongings. Indigenous people have also been displaced from their villages to the forests, or to areas contested by the army and rebel groups. Army 'scorched earth' operations have aimed to flush out people hiding in the jungle. Soldiers shoot on sight. Thousands of indigenous people have fled the country to become refugees.

Example 2: southern Sudan

Women and children are being enslaved in their thousands in war-torn Sudan. Most of them belong to the Dinka ethnic group, the largest in the south. Accurate figures are hard to come by, but since the civil war restarted in 1983, an estimated 14,000 Dinka people have been abducted. Between 5,000 and 14,000 slaves are still waiting to be released, many of them children. The victims mostly come from Bahr el Ghazal in the south, and the slave raiders from South Darfur and West Kordofan in northern Sudan. The men who do the raiding, and the families that keep Dinka women and children as slaves, belong to pastoralist groups called Baggara. They are cattle-herders, made up of Rizeigat and Misseriya people. The slaves are used for labor, both in the house and fields, and in some cases women and girls are forced to 'marry' their captors or their captors' relatives. Government officials tend to deny that kidnap victims who have been absorbed into family households are victims of slavery or human rights violations.

The Sudanese Government set up a Committee for the Eradication of Abduction of Women and Children (CEAWC) in 1999. It is supposed to end abductions, make sure that all victims of slavery return home safely, and punish anyone involved in abductions. But the trade has not stopped. Anti-Slavery International investigated CEAWC's work and found that progress has been very slow. It is urging the Government to state publicly that abductions and all associated practices are illegal, that those responsible will be prosecuted, and that slavery will not be tolerated.[9]

Language

Researchers have recently warned that 90 per cent of the world's languages, some of them spoken by indigenous peoples, could disappear by 2050.

It is the linguistic equivalent of an ecological disaster, say researchers at the University of Manchester, who held an 'endangered languages' day in May 2002. They aimed to raise awareness by playing tapes and videos of native speakers, and described their own investigative research around the world. One example of an endangered language is Tofa, spoken only by about 60 reindeer herders and hunters in central Siberia. Tofa has hardly ever been written down, but it has a rich oral tradition of epic poems, stories, proverbs and songs. In Turkey, the ban on education and broadcasts in Kurdish was finally lifted in 2002 after years of repression, as Turkey groomed itself for EU membership.

Languages are under threat because success, in many societies, can only be achieved through speaking and writing the dominant language, such as English or Russian. In many countries, indigenous or minority languages are banned in schools which follow a curriculum in the dominant, national language. Languages can only survive if they are passed from parents to children, and many parents are now choosing not to do so. 'Every language is the repository of the culture of the people who speak it,' says Nigel Vincent, Professor of Linguistics at the university. 'When we lose a language, we lose something of the world's diversity.'[10]

Health and disease

Indigenous peoples are vulnerable to diseases linked to poverty, including diabetes, heart and lung disease, malnutrition and HIV/AIDS. If little or no basic primary health care exists within reach, people die from easily preventable illness. Another factor is people's distrust of state health services, especially if they are staffed by whites or people who speak a different language. The sick may prefer to be treated with 'traditional' medicine in a more informal place. As a result of outside contact, people's diets have often changed for the worse, with sugary, processed, over-salted, additive- and pesticide-laced foods replacing the traditional ones. So they are now more vulnerable

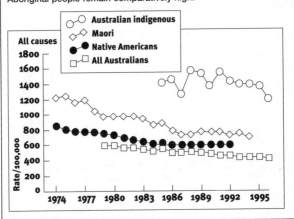

Mortality rates

Death rates from all causes for Maori and Native Americans have declined substantially since the 1970s, while those of Australian Aboriginal people remain comparatively high.

Reducing indigenous mortality in Australia: lessons from other countries by Ian T Ring and David Firmin. www.mja.com.au

to illnesses linked to Western diet.

There are high rates of alcoholism in some indigenous communities – a barometer of social breakdown, unemployment and despair. Drunkenness by non-whites is often used as an excuse for arrest and conviction, for example among Australian Aboriginals, who suffer disproportionately high rates of arrest for minor offences. Substance abuse is also on the rise, particularly petrol sniffing. A 1990 government inquiry showed that Aboriginal people are disproportionately likely to die from pneumonia, gastroenteritis, other diarrheal diseases, cirrhosis of the liver, pancreatitis, cot death and road accidents. Two white-introduced diseases – trachoma and leprosy – are still rife in Aboriginal communities years after they have disappeared in white ones.

There is a similar story in the Americas. Among Native Americans, the incidence of almost every known communicable disease is far higher compared with the population as a whole, infectious diseases are more likely to prove fatal, and alcoholism is the bane of many reservations. Tuberculosis rates in Canada

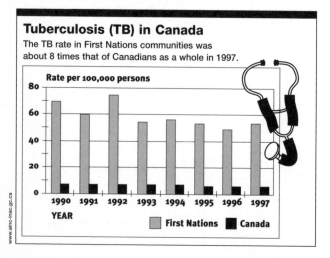

Tuberculosis (TB) in Canada

The TB rate in First Nations communities was about 8 times that of Canadians as a whole in 1997.

Rate per 100,000 persons

YEAR

First Nations ■ Canada

show a stark distinction between the health of the indigenous and non-indigenous populations.

HIV/AIDS is the 'new' scourge, largely affecting poor people in the South. It is impossible to give a breakdown of the numbers of indigenous peoples affected, because testing is not globally available and many people do not come forward anyway. But it is a particular danger in communities where women and girls are powerless to negotiate safe sex; in conflicts and refugee crises; where sex trafficking is rife; where traditional sexual practices are conducive to high rates of sexually transmitted disease; where there is increased urbanization and migrant labor movement; where mass tourism involves buying and selling sex alongside safaris, and where women desperate to feed their families may exchange sex for food.

The stolen children

To its infinite shame, the Australian Government once had a policy of forcibly taking Aboriginal children (particularly those of mixed-race) from their families and placing them in boarding schools or with white adoptive parents. It formed part of Australia's 'assimilation policy' in the 1950s and 1960s. These children became known as the 'stolen generations'. Lowitja O'Donoghue, first chair of the Aboriginal and Torres Strait Islander Commission and the first indigenous regional director for the country's Department of Aboriginal Affairs, described in a 1997 speech what it was like to be 'stolen':

'The moral issues are that it's not just family life that is disrupted by these policies – it's the whole sense of individual and community identity and the repercussions that are felt by later generations. I have personal experience of this.

In 1932... I was born at Granite Downs Station in the Pitjantjatjara lands in the north-west of South Australia. My father was an Irish station manager and my mother was a Yankunjatjara woman. When I was two years of age, I was taken from my mother and placed in the Colebrooke Home – a church mission in the town of Quorn in the Flinders Ranges – where my four sisters and one brother already lived.

None of us ever saw our father again. We were forbidden to speak our traditional language or to talk about our origins, and I learned a new culture and the new name that came with it – "Lois". As I grew older, I learned about our family from my brothers and sisters, and I resolved I would one day find our mother. It took me 30 years to achieve that goal, but it was supremely important for me to fulfil it. The problem was that when I did meet my mother again, we no longer had a common language and I was unable to speak with her.'

Being over-researched

The text below was specially written by Moronga Tanago, a member of the Bugakhwe San people of southern Africa, who is a board member of the Working Group of Indigenous Minorities in Southern Africa (WIMSA) working with TOCADI (Trust for Okavango Culture and Development Initiatives) on culture and education. He begins by talking about the wider problems faced by San people.

'It has been a great pleasure for me to have this opportunity to air my feelings as a San person about the problems that our people are facing. Though San people live right

across southern Africa, we all face similar problems. One of the biggest is the loss of our ancestral lands. Everywhere the San people have been pushed off or removed from their land by others... And the San have no power to fight this.

Because of their land loss the San people are the poorest in their countries, they struggle with education and with the problems other people brought, such as sickness and alcohol and drugs. But lately the other issue the San people are dealing with is that researchers have been studying them just for the sake of getting their PhDs. The San people feel that these researchers have been benefiting from the information they got from the San people, but the San do not feel as if they have benefited in any way from the information they have been giving out for such a long time. For example, some researchers worked on our languages or studied our ways of life, things which are very vital for us to use in future, and for the younger generation to know about. Unfortunately, we are often unable to access the information these researchers have taken from us because they write them in their own languages. Or when they write in ours they say it is too expensive to reproduce copies or books for our communities.

The very important point that I would like to share is that people must understand that we, the San, are now organized. We have our own organizations and networks that link us across the countries we live in. WIMSA networks with other San organizations in the region. The organization I work for is part of this network and others.

Honestly, the San are only asking any person who does research or who wants to write about us, film us or use our cultural goods in any way, to respect these networks and contact us through WIMSA, because we now have policies and a contract for media and research purposes. In fact, people who fail to do so will in future not receive any help or agreement from San communities. Our main aim is that the San should also benefit from the information they give out and the hospitality they have offered to other people over so many years. We are not only talking about books, copies of films, tapes etc., but also information that we can use to strengthen ourselves to hold out against the pressures of the modern times and the *politics in our countries. We want to see that information work for us. This is the last chance for the San to preserve something of our own identity and knowledge, since we have lost so much of it already through our contact with other people. I hope that anyone who reads this piece will enjoy knowing more about us, but also face the challenges that we lay before you.'*[11]

Indigenous peoples are not simply victims, as Moronga makes abundantly clear. The next chapter describes some of the vibrant resistance movements, past and present, and people's individual and collective achievements on the road to rights for all.

1 From an 'Open Letter to the Canadian People' by Barabaig leaders, quoted in *Pastures Lost*, (Charles Lane, Initiatives Publishers 1996). **2** Adapted from Lane, *Pastures Lost*. Thanks to Virginia Luling for additional information. **3** Partly adapted from accounts by Survival International, which has campaigned for and with the Yanomami since the 1970s, and other web sources such as: www.crystalinks.com/yanomami **4** Based, with the author's permission, on a paper by Dr Ben Knighton. **5** From 'A history of resistance to central government control', in a series of reports on repression of Montagnards, Human Rights Watch, viewable at www.hrw.org/reports/2002/vietnam **6** Written for this book by Sue Wheat of Tourism Concern. For guidance on community-run holidays, see Tourism Concern's new guidebook, *The Good Alternative Travel Guide* (Earthscan 2002). **7** Lynn Barber, 'How Machu Picchu left me on a high', *The Observer*, 25 November 2001. **8** From a case study in John Beauclerk and Jeremy Narby with Janet Townsend, *Indigenous Peoples: a fieldguide for development* (Oxfam 1988). **9** From 'Forced labor and slavery of women and children in Sudan (27-31 May 2002)' and 'Slavery in Sudan (11-15 June 2001)', UN Commission on Human Rights. Viewable at www.antislavery.org **10** From David Ward, 'Language cull could leave people speechless', *The Guardian*, 25 May 2002. **11** See Contacts p 139 for WIMSA's contact details.

5 Fighting back

Protest and resistance over the centuries... The struggle continues today on many fronts... local and global, and links to worldwide protest against globalization... a look at some protest movements, past and present, and the folk heroes who have led or lead the struggle now.

ON 25 JUNE 1876, above the Little Bighorn River in what is today Montana, a force of Lakota and Cheyenne warriors destroyed General George Custer and 255 soldiers of the US Seventh Cavalry in what has been called 'the last great Indian triumph in American history'.[1] The battle of Little Bighorn – Custer's Last Stand – is possibly the most famous clash ever between whites and Native Americans, if not between Europeans and indigenous peoples anywhere. Psychologically, it was a coup, the indigenous equivalent of David beating Goliath. Inevitably, however, it led to a vicious payback: white leaders and soldiers vowed to wipe out the 'Indian'. There was a similar story across colonial Africa, where many indigenous and tribal peoples tried to resist Europeans with spears and arrows, only to be brutally put down in most cases. Military tit for tat rarely leads to real victory in the end. Violent protest has had its uses but it should not overshadow the many other forms of indigenous resistance that have been used with mixed success before and since.

The Aborigines' Protection Society (APS) was launched in London in 1837 by prominent abolitionists of slavery who realized that emancipation had not cured the problem of European exploitation of indigenous peoples. The first African branch (called the Aborigines' Rights Protection Society, ARPS) was set up in the Gold Coast (now Ghana), West Africa, in 1897. Similar African groups followed. In the early days, 'Aborigine' simply referred to non-whites, and not necessarily First Peoples. The two great features of these organizations in Africa were that they provided an alternative route to London for complainants, who could get inconvenient questions asked about the treatment of colonized Africans by sympathetic members of parliament. The official route was no good because it went through the colonial hierarchy. Second, their very existence gave hope to colonized peoples and those who sided with them. Even in countries where there were no branches, such as South Africa, a network of correspondents kept London informed. Some of these whistle-blowers were themselves colonial officials. The APS largely concentrated on the colonies, while the closely linked British and Foreign Anti-Slavery Society (founded 1839) dealt with territories outside the empire. In 1909, they merged to become the Anti-Slavery and Aborigines' Protection Society, the crusading organization today called Anti-Slavery International.[2]

Much earlier, in the US, indigenous leaders used formal legal channels to assert their rights to land. The Mohegan land case, for example, went to the Privy Council in London in 1765. The Mohegan were struggling to reclaim lands illegally seized by the colony of Connecticut. Their spokesperson, Samson Occom, toured Britain for two years from 1765, preaching 300 sermons and raising more than £12,000 for the cause. Unhappily for them, the Privy Council dismissed the case. In 1833, a Pequot 'Indian' preacher and writer, William Apess, led the Mashpee Revolt in protest against the unfair laws of Massachusetts. The Mashpee won most of their demands, and Apess became a national figure. Other later legal cases included the unsuccessful eight-year court battle by the Montauk Indians from Long Island, launched in 1909. They wanted to regain their land title and keep developers out. The developers argued that the Montauk were no longer an 'Indian tribe' because they had intermarried with African-Americans and taken up a modern lifestyle. The judge agreed, and threw the case out.

Back in Africa, colonial Kenya was the scene of an extraordinary case brought by the Maasai in 1913. With the help of British lawyers, they took the British Government to court to challenge the legality of land snatching and win reparations for land and stock losses suffered during a forced move (see **Folk hero**: Ole Gilisho p 96). Again, they lost on a flimsy pretext – but their battle continues today. Using new evidence, and spearheaded by Maasai lawyers this time around, they plan to bring another action against Britain in the international courts to challenge this 100-year-old injustice. They will be encouraged by a victory scored by Maasai and Samburu from northern Kenya in July 2002. The British Ministry of Defence agreed to pay £4.5 million compensation plus legal costs to 228 pastoralists who were bereaved or injured by British army explosives left lying around on their grazing land after military exercises.

In the colonial period, indigenous and tribal peoples took to litigation after petitions and other peaceful means failed. Early petitions and delegations

---

Folk hero: Bruce McGuinness, Australia

In the late 1960s and 1970s he was an important leader of the Black Power Movement among Aboriginal people, which was instrumental in politicizing indigenous Australia. As the first Aboriginal Director of the Aborigines Advancement League (AAL), he introduced the term Black Power to Australia. He was among the instigators of the Aboriginal Embassy (see p 101) and played a major role in the ensuing struggle for Aboriginal control over Aboriginal affairs. McGuinness became chair of the National Aboriginal Consultative Committee, later took a lead in creating community-controlled health services across the country, and helped to set up the National Aboriginal and Islander Health Organization which spearheaded political agitation in the 1980s. His talents also span the arts and media. His 1972 radio show on Melbourne's ZZZ station was the first regular radio program for indigenous Australians. The same year, he wrote and directed the first film made by an Aboriginal person, *Black Fire*. In 1974, he made the historical movie *A Time to Dream*. ∎

You can visit his website at www.kooriweb.org/bbm
Adapted from a profile by Gary Foley at
www.kooriweb.org/foley/heroes2.html

Some landmark dates for the indigenous movement

(IP = indigenous peoples)

1920s Alaskan Native Brotherhood and Society for American Indians formed

1923 Indigenous leader Deskaheh, from the Iroquois Confederacy, unsuccessfully seeks help from the League of Nations, Geneva, in their dispute with the Canadian government

1957 ILO Convention 107, first international instrument covering IP – but no IP were consulted in the drafting

1968 International Work Group for Indigenous Affairs (IWGIA) set up

1974-5 American Indian Treaty Council established in the US (now called International Indian Treaty Council)

1977 World Council of Indigenous Peoples set up, Canada; First international NGO conference on IP issues, Geneva

1982 UN establishes Working Group on Indigenous Populations

1984 Coordinating Body for Indigenous Organizations of the Amazon Basin (COICA) formed

1986 India launches its first Tribal and Indigenous Council

1989 ILO Convention 169 replaces the 1957 Convention

1992 UN Conference on Environment and Development (UNCED): the Rio Declaration recognizes indigenous peoples' role in environmental protection

1992 Asia Indigenous Peoples Pact formed to represent Asian IP

1992 Rigoberta Menchú (Maya Indian from Guatemala) wins Nobel Peace Prize

1993 World Conference on Human Rights: the Vienna Declaration and Programme of Action recommend that the UN General Assembly proclaim the Decade, establish the Permanent Forum on Indigenous Issues and adopt a declaration on indigenous rights

1993 The UN General Assembly proclaims the UN International Decade of the World's Indigenous Peoples

1995-2004 UN International Decade of the World's Indigenous Peoples

1998 The UN Commission on Human Rights sets up the Ad-Hoc Working Group on the establishment of the Permanent Forum

2000 Permanent Forum on Indigenous Issues established

May 2002 First meeting of the Permanent Forum, New York

to London included those by Maori to Queen Victoria before the 1840 Waitangi Treaty, when they complained about the damage being done to Maori land and culture by settlers and land speculators. Aborigines on Flinders Island in the Bass Strait petitioned the Queen in 1846. Lobengula, king of the Ndebele in what is now Zimbabwe, sent two representatives to London in 1889 to beg for protection against land grabbers and gold diggers led by Cecil Rhodes. They returned with royal greetings, but no protection. The Griqua of South Africa also appealed for British protection in the 1860s, in the face of a land takeover by diamond miners. This failed, and they rebelled in 1878. Swazi envoys went to London in 1894 to ask Queen Victoria to protect Swaziland against the Boers; their petition was also refused. A series of petitions and delegations by South African chiefs to King George V in the 1900s asked him to veto aggressive new laws that took land and rights away from black people.

The indigenous movement really took off in the 1960s and 1970s. Its rapid growth coincided with the independence struggles of colonized peoples, decolonization, the rise of Red Power in North America and Black Power in the US and Australia in particular, the flowering of the human rights movement and of the UN. The movement became increasingly international, with the setting up of the International Indian Treaty Council in 1974 in the US and the World Council of Indigenous Peoples in 1977 in Canada. These two bodies helped to initiate the first international conference of non-governmental organizations (NGOs) on indigenous issues in 1977 in Geneva, which effectively launched the global indigenous movement. The last two decades of the 20th century saw a groundswell of politicized indigenous activity across Africa, South America, Asia, the Pacific and elsewhere, linked to the explosion of civil society organizations (CSOs) among the world's poor, and the declining power of some states.[3]

Folk hero: Rigoberta Menchú Tum, Guatemala

Rigoberta Menchú is a Mayan-Quiche activist who was awarded the Nobel Peace Prize in 1992, the youngest person and the first indigenous person ever to receive it. Besides promoting peace she has fought all her life for indigenous and women's rights, global education and universal justice. Despite little schooling, Rigoberta was politically active from an early age – as soon as she was old enough to accompany her father to meetings of a local peasant activists' group. Her resolve deepened after her parents and two brothers were tortured and killed by the military in the early 1980s, during a time of government crackdown on 'communist guerrillas'. Rigoberta had to flee to Mexico, where she spoke out against repression in Guatemala. She gave talks across the Americas, calling for peace in her country and justice for indigenous peoples. She has raised global awareness of the issues, and set up a foundation to promote peace, indigenous rights and other causes. ∎

Adapted from a profile on Cultural Survival's Ethnosphere website.

Today, many of the protests link to anti-globalization campaigning. The collective enemy now is the kind of modern imperialism that forces its agenda, values, armies, bombs and products on other societies. Indigenous protest also feeds into other types of wider activism, such as the Landless Workers' Movement (MST) in Brazil and the 'nuclear free' movement in the Pacific. But globalization in its broadest sense also has its uses, since indigenous protesters are increasingly using the internet to make contacts, link up, and put pressure on governments and the corporate sector. A wealth of information about indigenous peoples' protest movements is available on the web. It is fast, furious and successful – making up for past losses, when a lack of literacy and access to technology meant that many protests went unheard.

One of the hot issues you can read about on the web is the call for the repatriation of human remains and other artifacts stolen from indigenous peoples.

Bones of contention

Museums are coming under increasing pressure to

give up their collections of indigenous human remains. Many acquired these collections in the Victorian and Edwardian eras, when travelers, scientists and trophy-hunters collected bodies and body parts from far-flung places to put on display in the West. Indigenous groups want the body parts returned home for a decent burial.

In Britain, a government working group is now considering the issues, after requests from the Australian Government and indigenous peoples' groups. There have long been calls for the return of such treasures as the Elgin marbles to Greece and Benin bronzes, but the dead are a different class altogether because their display is obviously offensive and upsetting to the living. Museums are also uneasy about the dubious way in which they got these collections. For example, the Natural History Museum in London has 20,000 body parts including a skull and leg bone from a young man who was shot in 1900 near Victoria River, Australia, during a so-called punitive raid. The collector 'prepared' the bones on the spot, boiling off the skin in a cooking pot.

Some European institutions have begun to repatriate remains without waiting for the law to change. In May 2002 the Royal College of Surgeons of England, in London, began to return all its Tasmanian collections, including the skin and hair of Truganini – one of the last Aboriginal Tasmanians and a campaigner for her people (see chapter 2). The French Government has recently returned the skeleton of Saartjie Baartman, a Khoisan woman known as the Hottentot Venus, who suffered years of humiliation being put on show as a freak in Europe. The skull of Yagan, an Australian warrior shot and beheaded in 1833, was exhumed in 1997 from a Liverpool cemetery where it had been buried by a local museum in the 1960s. The remains of Native Americans Chief Long Wolf and Star were disinterred from a London cemetery in 1997 and returned to the US.

But indigenous protesters are concerned that many museums still have narrow criteria for returning remains, oppose repatriation, or have no policy on it at all. They welcome what is happening in Britain. 'Recent developments have seen repatriation move into the political sphere, a progression which mirrors that which occurred in Australia and the US 10 to 15 years ago,' say activists Cressida Fforde and Lyndon Ormond Parker. 'This is what forced the scientific and museum community to accept that they no longer had sole rights to decide what should happen to indigenous human

Mayagna Indian victory over the Nicaraguan Government

In September 2001, the Inter-American Court of Human Rights (IACHR) declared that Nicaragua had violated the human rights of the Mayagna Indian community in Awas Tingni, on the country's Atlantic coast, and ordered the Government to recognize and protect the community's legal rights to its traditional lands, natural resources and environment. The decision has far-reaching implications.

'It is precedent-setting internationally,' says James Anaya, special counsel to the US-based Indian Law Resource Center (ILRC) which represents the community and helped bring the case to court. 'Members of the community have fought for decades to protect their land and resources and against government neglect and encroachment by loggers. This decision vindicates the rights they have struggled so long to protect.'

There are many similar land and resource disputes across the Americas, but this is the first of its kind to be addressed by the IACHR. It was filed after the Nicaraguan legal system had failed this community. Under international law, governments must respect indigenous peoples' rights to their traditional land. But if a government does not demarcate such land, their territorial rights remain uncertain. Anaya says the Nicaraguan Government exploited this confusion, granting foreign companies licenses to log much of the tropical forest where the community lives. Now it must respect indigenous land rights. The court ordered the Government to demarcate the Awas Tingni community's traditional lands, demarcate the lands of all indigenous groups in the country, and pay $50,000 compensation as well as all legal costs. ∎

From Amazon Alliance for Indigenous and Traditional Peoples of the Amazon Basin. http://www.amazonalliance.org

remains in their collections.' Activists also demand increased access to collection documentation – something many museums are wary of. Without being able to see the archives, indigenous communities cannot find out whose remains are being held. The question of what to do with remains whose origin is unclear is one of the biggest problems around repatriation.

Within Australia, there have been major restitutions since the Government adopted national policies on repatriating remains. The main one is the Strategic Plan for the Return of Indigenous Ancestral Remains, unveiled in 1998, which does not apply to collections overseas. In the US, repatriation is largely covered by the Native American Graves Protection and Repatriation Act (NAGPRA), 1990. It protects burial sites on federal and tribal lands and creates a process for repatriating cultural items, including artifacts and human remains, to 'tribes'. In 1993, museums holding Native American artifacts were ordered to make written summaries of their collections for distribution to people culturally linked to the artifacts; in 1995, they were told to make detailed inventories. These and other developments have increased tensions between Native American activists, academics and archeologists. The ongoing rows include arguments over Kennewick Man, a 9,200-year-old body found in Kennewick, Washington, in 1996. Should scientists be allowed to study his remains, or should he be allowed to rest in peace on Native American land?[4]

Land struggles: Ogiek, Kenya

In Kenya, Ogiek people are fighting attempts by their own government to evict them from the Mau forests to the west of the Rift Valley. Hunter-gatherers who claim to have lived in these forests for centuries, the 20,000-strong Ogiek have taken the Government to court over the future of the Mau forests. If evicted, the Ogiek face destitution. Government plans for the Mau area are part of its plans to 'de-gazette' four per cent of Kenya's forests. These would open up the forests to squatters as well as logging companies and other private business ventures. The Government accuses the Ogiek of failing to protect young trees. Community leaders retort that it is invaders, deliberately brought onto their land by politicians, who have been destroying and logging the forests. It is alleged that President Moi's government, with elections in December 2002,was 'buying' support by parceling out tracts of forest land.

The Ogiek people are being backed by local and global environmentalists and pressure groups. Besides the threat to the Ogiek, these official plans also threaten the environment – state-sponsored deforestation has already wreaked havoc with water supplies in a country regularly ravaged by drought. The latest news is that the court case has been adjourned yet again.[5]

Ogoni victory in Nigeria

An African commission has recently ruled that the Nigerian Government must compensate the Ogoni people for abuses caused by oil production and state security forces. It must also clean up lands and rivers that have been damaged by oil pollution.

Campaigners hail the ruling by the African Commission on Human and People's Rights as affirming so-called ESC rights: economic, social and cultural. It is a major breakthrough in the battle for international recognition of such rights, which are usually rated lower than political and civil rights, particularly by Western states. The case was filed by a Lagos-based human rights group soon after the execution in November 1995 of nine leaders of the Movement for the Survival of the Ogoni People (MOSOP). The victims included the world famous writer Ken Saro-wiwa. MOSOP and Saro-wiwa had led a global campaign to raise awareness of the plight of the Ogoni, a minority people living in the oil-rich Niger Delta. They claimed that their lands had been polluted for years as a result of operations by Shell and the national petroleum company, NNPC. Protests in the early 1990s brought vicious military repression; scores of people were killed and villages razed. Shell became the target of an international consumer boycott after the executions, and Nigeria faced sanctions that were only lifted after the return to civilian rule in 1999. Now it is hoped that this important human rights ruling will influence other states. ∎

Adapted from 'People versus Big Oil' by Jim Lobe, 5 July 2002, at www.pfip.org/commentary/2002/0207nigeria.html

Land and related struggles: Colombia

There are about half a million indigenous people in Colombia, belonging to some 81 different ethnic groups. The country's 334 indigenous reserves are home to 83.5 per cent of the indigenous population. But reserve boundaries are not clearly defined, land titles overlap with those of non-indigenous landowners, non-indigenous settlers have come in and there is not enough land to support everybody. In some places, drug-traffickers, supported by the security forces, have tried to grab large tracts of land. When indigenous people have peacefully defended their territory, they have been arrested and ill-treated. Whole communities have been violently evicted and indigenous leaders jailed for 'trespass'.

Amnesty International says some attempts to evict indigenous communities have resulted in deliberate killings. Also, the army often accuses indigenous people of collaborating with anti-government guerrillas. Many have been arrested, tortured and killed by soldiers and paramilitaries. Indigenous community leaders who refuse to collaborate with the guerrillas have also been intimidated and in some cases murdered. Recent human rights violations resulting from land conflict include the massacre of 20 Paez Indians in December 1991 by police and paramilitaries. The victims had been occupying a ranch called El Nilo in southern Colombia. In the months leading up to the killings, the Paez had complained to the authorities about the way the new ranch owner (rumored to be involved in drug-trafficking) was threatening them. Investigators later found strong evidence that the local police commander and anti-narcotics chief were among those behind the massacre, but charges were dropped. In December 1993, Paez leaders went on hunger strike to demand that the president honor his pledge that justice would be done. They ended their strike after being assured this would happen. The two accused police chiefs carried on working for

several years. Seven civilians, including the landown-
er, paramilitary men and drug-traffickers, were
eventually sentenced to 30 years' imprisonment for
their role in the killings, but by 1997, the authorities
said it was not possible to take any further action
against others. Several lawyers representing the Paez
in this and other land cases have been assassinated;
others have received death threats. The Paez are still
waiting for justice.[6]

Struggle for self-rule: the Kurds

The Kurds, who are scattered across Turkey, Iraq, Iran
and Syria, have long struggled for a Kurdish state – but
Kurdistan still only exists in the imagination. They are

Fighting over Fiji

Every ethnic group in Fiji is descended from immigrants. Racial strife
has broken out over competing claims to indigenousness, and the right
of particular groups to run the country. Some say that upholding the
rights of one group is all well and good, so long as other peoples' rights
are not thereby extinguished or trampled upon. Indigenous Fijians say
that self-identification and the right to self-determination go hand in
hand. But should self-identification as indigenous allow certain communities total freedom to rule over and even terrorize others? This
example shows how fraught the whole subject can be.

In May 2000 a failed businessman called George Speight led a coup
here. He overthrew the multi-racial and left-leaning government of
Mahendra Chaudhry, and he and his gunmen held the cabinet hostage
for 56 days inside the parliament building. Speight claimed that
Chaudhry, an ethnic Fijian Indian, had no right to rule over indigenous
Fijians. Speight was arrested and pleaded guilty to treason; his death
sentence was later commuted to life imprisonment. Speight is hailed as
a hero by other indigenous peoples in the region, though Chaudhry has
claimed that rightwing forces and big business interests were behind
the coup, not indigenous rights. The coup and its aftermath have left
Fijians wondering: who is really indigenous here, and how many centuries will it take before the so-called immigrant races (Indo-Fijians,
Chinese and Europeans) become 'natives'?

Native Fijians are the biggest ethnic group, forming more than half
the population. They are said to be descendants of the great chief
Lutunasobasoba, who led his people across the seas in a giant canoe
to Fiji. It is not clear where they came from. The first Europeans to set-

one of the world's largest ethnic groups without their own state. Now the US-led 'war on terrorism' seems to be strangling Kurdish aspirations for nationhood. The Kurdistan Workers' Party (PKK) has been added to a European Union list of banned 'terrorist' organizations, though in Turkey it had begun putting away its guns and transforming itself into a political movement. Some leaders say this ban criminalizes the whole of the Kurdish people. Since the Gulf War, the 3.5 million Kurds in northern Iraq have enjoyed limited regional self-rule in the UN 'safe haven'. But an uneasy peace reigns so long as Saddam Hussein remains in power. Saddam's forces have bombed, napalmed, murdered and terrorized Iraqi Kurds. In

tle were shipwrecked sailors and runaway convicts from Australian penal colonies. By the mid-19th century, they were joined by sandalwood traders and missionaries. The Lauans, who are descended from Tongans, settled from 1848 onwards with their chief Ma'afu. From 1879 to 1916, Indians arrived as indentured laborers to work on the sugar plantations. The islands were ceded to Britain in 1874.

But native Fijians do not entirely meet the definitions of indigenousness outlined in chapter 1. They descend from people who lived here before colonization and before other ethnic groups arrived, but they are not non-dominant and non-state actors. Their culture, institutions and language are not entirely separate from and alien to the national ones; for example, indigenous Fijian culture is the dominant one on state occasions. With regard to the IWGIA definitions, they are not disadvantaged and have never suffered dispossession, discrimination or political marginalization (though people do not cease to be indigenous just because they have gained some political and economic power). In fact, they dominate Fijian political and economic life, and native chiefs communally own 83 per cent of the land. So some say it is absurd to liken the position of native Fijians today to that of other oppressed indigenous groups such as Aboriginal Australians. If anything, lawyers claim that it is the minorities here (Indo-Fijians, Chinese, Europeans and others) who need constitutional safeguards against violation of their rights. At the end of the day, many Fijians are asking: whatever happened to racial equality? ■

Based on a paper by Victor Lal, an Oxford-based Fijian lawyer and writer. For an alternative overview, see IWGIA, *The Indigenous World 2000-2001*.

Folk hero: Parsaloi Ole Gilisho, Kenya

Ole Gilisho was an unsung African Geronimo. In 1911-13, when he was an illiterate warrior, he led a peaceful rebellion against the British colonial Government that was trying to force the pastoralist Maasai people out of their ancestral lands into reserves to make way for white settlers. The British expected violent resistance. Instead, Ole Gilisho surprised them by hiring British lawyers and, with the help of a British doctor called Norman Leys, took the Government to court to challenge the forced moves and land losses. The so-called Maasai Case of 1913 was lost on a technicality. But it was a landmark legal action for its time and place – probably the first time indigenous peoples in this part of Africa had challenged the legality of colonial oppression and land snatching. The Maasai lost the case and up to 70 per cent of their land. But Ole Gilisho is remembered today as a selfless hero who put the welfare of his beloved people first, and used modern legal processes to take on the colonizers. ■

the late 1980s they destroyed more than 4,000 villages and 20 towns, and sowed countless landmines in the countryside, forcing thousands of families into crumbling cities. In 1988 they used chemical weapons to attack Halabjah, killing between 4,000 and 7,000 people. This atrocity is still claiming Kurdish lives today.

Now, with the US threatening to attack Iraq again, Iraqi Kurds anxiously wonder if this is going to help their cause. Washington has reportedly put pressure on them to provide frontline fighters. Would rising in support of a US bid to topple Saddam make things any better, or destroy what they have? 'We have been let down before,' says former rebel fighter Sherwan Mohammed from Sulaymaniyah. 'Who is to say it won't happen again?' Under UN protection, the Kurds are better off than Iraqis living in Government-controlled territory further south. Towns, schools and hospitals have been rebuilt with aid money and oil revenues, and landmines are being cleared. They have not felt the full force of UN sanctions against Iraq, which have led to widespread misery and death. But Kurdish leaders demand that the US and its allies, second time around, must support a democratic government to replace Saddam's regime, and guarantee their security in Kurdish-run territory. A separate state remains a dream.[7]

Struggle for self-rule: the Kanaks

The Kanaks are what indigenous Melanesian people call themselves. On the islands of Kanaky (New Caledonia) in the Pacific, they have been struggling to throw off the colonial yoke ever since the French annexed the islands in 1853. A French military regime ruled New Caledonia for the rest of the century. Colonialism was a bitter experience. Dispossessed of their lands and decimated, the Kanaks became a powerless 'minority' in their own land, even though they make up about 44 per cent of the population today. They did not get the right to vote until 1957. The struggle continues over land and political power, and has become increasingly violent.

Kanaky/New Caledonia is still a French Overseas Territory. 1984-86 saw political turmoil and violence, known simply as 'The Events'. Independence parties, disillusioned by the French Government's empty promises for reform, launched the FLNKS (Front de Libération National Kanak et Socialiste). Its first leader was Jean-Marie Tjibaou. Violence broke out when the FLNKS boycotted the 1984 election, and one of its leaders was shot by paramilitaries. France flew in

---

Treaty success in Canada

Indigenous peoples in Canada won a landmark ruling after a marathon parliament session in December 1999. The 42-hour session came about when the opposition Reform Party tabled 471 amendments in a bid to halt a treaty that gives land and extended rights to the descendants of First Peoples. The treaty, which was 20 years in the making, gives the 5,500 remaining Nisga'a people around 2,000 square kilometers of land in British Columbia, a share of the Nass River salmon stocks, and also self-government. They were set to receive $330 million in benefits and cash. But it was a trade-off: in return they agreed to give up all rights to future land claims and lost their tax-exempt status. Some indigenous groups have criticized the treaty for being too moderate. ■

---

troops and declared a six-month state of emergency. In 1986 the UN put Kanaky back on its decolonization list, which gave hope to the independence movement. But France accused the UN of meddling in its internal affairs and expelled the Australian consul general from the islands, saying he had played a leading role in this. Tjibaou was assassinated in 1989 by a splinter group of Kanaks who claimed that the FLNKS had sold out. The Nouméa Accords of 1998 have delayed independence until 2013 at the earliest.[8]

Trick or treaty?

Some colonial treaties were not entirely bad news for indigenous peoples, since they recognized indigenous sovereignty. These can sometimes be used today to win reparations and prove separate nationhood. But others (such as the Waitangi Treaty made between the British and the Maori in 1840) specifically took indigenous sovereignty away and vested it in the Crown. It marked the start of massive land losses, leaving Maori with 1.6 million hectares of land out of pre-colonial holdings of 25 million. Even so, the Maori have managed to use the treaty to regain some of their rights, for it guaranteed them 'full exclusive and undisturbed possession of their lands and estates forests fisheries and other properties'. The Waitangi Tribunal was established in 1975 as a permanent commission of inquiry into Maori claims relating to the treaty.

In the US, 371 treaties were signed with Native Americans up to 1871. Numerous legal challenges have followed. There are some parallels with Aotearoa/New Zealand; for example, the Fort Laramie Treaty of 1868 guaranteed certain rights to Native Americans, including lands being set apart for their exclusive and undisturbed use. Some groups have successfully used this since to try and regain their losses. This treaty, which the defendants fought to present as evidence in court, was a major theme at the trials following the taking of Wounded Knee by members of the American Indian Movement in 1973.[9]

Making a stand

Other kinds of protest have sought to expose injustice and racism generally, using methods that embarrass governments, hold up a mirror to society and take their cue from the American civil rights movement and Black Power. Here are two examples of indigenous Australian activism:

The Freedom Ride

This took place in 1965, when former soccer player and University of Sydney student Charles Perkins decided to expose the high levels of segregation and racism rampant in New South Wales at that time. Perkins and the Reverend Ted Noffs organized a Freedom Ride with 30 white university students from the group Student Action for Aborigines (SAFA). They took a bus to visit the state's most racist country towns. They were pelted with eggs and rotten fruit when they tried to desegregate a swimming pool. The

---

Folk hero: Evo Morales, Bolivia

Coca-chewing indigenous leader Evo Morales came tantalizingly close to becoming president of Bolivia in 2002. An Aymara Indian, son of a peasant farmer and socialist leader of Bolivia's coca-growers, he was by July 2002 running neck and neck with millionaire businessman Gonzalo Sanchez de Lozada (the eventual winner) despite having launched his campaign with an approval rating of just 3 per cent. But since neither man won an absolute majority at the polls, the country's Congress had to decide – and elected Lozada by 84 votes to 43. Morales had called for the 'Yankees' to be kicked out, for Bolivia to default on debt, to nationalize industry and put peasant communes in charge of running mines, railways and electricity companies. He especially upset the US by opposing its plans to end coca growing; the US threatened to withdraw aid if Morales was made president. The US-funded coca eradication program has wiped out 50,000 hectares of crop, and is hated because many poor people claim it has made them even poorer. Morales calls it a violation of Bolivian sovereignty. ∎

hired bus driver felt so intimidated he quit the tour halfway through. But the resulting publicity raised awareness around the world, exposing Australian racism in the raw. This event set the scene for a pattern of protest that continued and expanded during the 1970s and 1980s, and inspired a whole generation to stand up for their rights. Activist Gary Foley, now Senior Curator of the Indigenous Cultures Program at Museum Victoria in Melbourne, was one of those it inspired. He says of its long-term significance: 'The Freedom Ride represents the beginning of a more radical (and effective) form of protest in the Australian indigenous struggle. A whole new genera-tion of young indigenous political activists were

---

Folk hero: Geronimo, North America

Also known as Goyathlay (pronounced Goyahkla and meaning 'one who yawns'), Geronimo is remembered as a formidable warrior and survivor who waged many battles with the US military. He was one of several outstanding leaders of the Apache people, among the first and last tribes to resist white encroachment. Born in 1829 in what is today Western New Mexico, he lost his entire family – including his mother, young wife Alope and three children – when Mexican troops attacked their camp. This mass murder, in the 1850s, led to a burn-ing desire for vengeance and Geronimo's life-long hatred of Mexicans. Ironically, it was Mexican soldiers who gave him the name Geronimo, now synonymous with indigenous struggle. He played cat and mouse with a US Government agent called John Clum, who was obsessed with the idea of arresting and hanging the 'troublemaker'. On many occasions, when the noose was tightening around him, he miraculously threw off his pursuers and escaped from under their noses. In 1875 all Apaches west of the Rio Grande were ordered into a reservation. Geronimo escaped from the reservation three times and always managed to avoid capture. A shaman, he believed he had been given special powers to resist the white man's weapons; he certainly survived many gunshot wounds and held out the longest of all Native Americans. He died in Alabama in 1909 as a prisoner of war, unable to return to his homeland. When he surrendered in 1886, Geronimo said: 'Once I moved about like the wind. Now I surrender to you and that is all… My heart is yours and I hope yours will be mine.' ■

His autobiography is viewable on the web. 'Geronimo: His own story', part of the American Revolution project at http://odur.rug.nl

inspired by the Freedom Ride and they went on to form the nucleus of the group that established the Aboriginal Embassy.'

The Aboriginal Embassy

On 27 January 1972, four indigenous activists pitched a beach umbrella on the lawns outside Parliament House, Canberra, and proclaimed the site the 'Aboriginal Embassy'. They declared that a statement made by Prime Minister McMahon the day before – in which he had promised dilute action to review and improve the position of Aboriginal people in Australia – had effectively relegated indigenous people to the status of 'aliens in our own land'. Therefore, as aliens, they had decided to have an embassy of their own. They expected the police swiftly to evict them. But by chance, they had hit on a loophole in the law. There was no law against camping on the lawns of Parliament House so long as there were less than twelve tents.

The four – Billy Craigie, Tony Coorey, Michael Anderson and Bert Williams – soon caught the imagination of Australia. Within days they had set up an office tent and a letterbox. Mail began pouring in. Tourist operators saw the site as a new attraction and began bringing busloads of tourists to the 'embassy'. People donated money, brought food and blankets, and invited the 'embassy staff' – now swelled by other activists – home for showers and dinner. The mass media lapped it all up. The Aboriginal Embassy very quickly became the most successful protest venture yet launched by the Aboriginal political movement. The 'embassy' issued a series of demands, which included a call for Aboriginal control of the Northern Territory and minimum compensation of at least Aus$ 6 billion (US$ 3.4 billion) and a percentage of the gross national-al product for alienated lands. Opposition leader Gough Whitlam paid a formal visit, and declared that a Labor Government would reverse McMahon Government policies towards Aboriginal people. This was a major breakthrough for the Black Power activists at the core of the protest action.

The tent embassy could not last. The Government changed the law and sent nearly 100 police in to arrest the demonstrators. But important points had been made, and the Government thoroughly embarrassed. Not least, the televised scenes of over-the-top police violence brought a strong public response. On 30 July more than 2,000 indigenous people and their supporters staged the biggest land rights demonstration in the history of Canberra. There was a government-convened national conference of indigenous representatives, which called for the 'embassy' to be re-established. Next, the Supreme Court declared the Trespass on Commonwealth Lands Ordinance – under which the 'trespassers' had been evicted – was invalid. The 'embassy' was put up again while the Government rushed through more laws. But by now its reputation and credibility on indigenous affairs was in tatters. It lost the next election in a Labor landslide, ending 22 years of conservative rule.

In helping to destabilize the McMahon Government, the Aboriginal Embassy protest helped to change the course of Australian history. Activists say its most enduring effect was to influence the moderates in the indigenous struggle. Legendary Sydney Aboriginal community matriarch Shirley Smith has said of her experience: 'If I was going to think of a sign along the road that marked for me the beginning of militant Black Power politics, that sign would have printed on it – Aboriginal Embassy.'[10]

And in September 2002, news broke that opposition by Aboriginal Mirrar people had halted mining giant Rio Tinto's plans to develop the Jabiluka uranium mine in Australia's Northern Territory. The victory crowned more than five years of Mirrar protest, which climaxed in demonstrations at the Johannesburg 'Earth Summit', in August that year.

Intellectual property and biopiracy

Theft of intellectual property, traditional knowledge and biological/genetic resources (biopiracy) have been called a new form of colonization. For one thing, biotechnology companies are busy patenting plant varieties without compensating local farmers, therefore depriving them of the produce of their own sweat. This also involves theft from past generations, since it was they whose lifelong experimentation in the field helped to improve plant varieties. Farmers are banned from planting patented seeds without paying for the 'privilege', and so-called terminator technology has been developed to stop seeds germinating when replanted, which leaves farmers at the mercy of seed producers. All this threatens local food security and biodiversity, as well as the very survival of small farmers. But the biotechs are not stopping at plants: living beings, micro-organisms, animals and even human

Folk hero: Eddie Mabo, Australia

Eddie Koiki Mabo (1936-92) was a Torres Strait Islander who fought to challenge unjust white laws. The historic 1992 Mabo Decision by Australia's High Court overturned the notion of *terra nullius* or no one's land, which the British had declared when laying claim to the country. The court ruled that the Murray Islanders who had brought the case, led by Eddie, were entitled to possess, occupy, use and enjoy their lands. Unhappily, Eddie did not live to see victory; he had died of cancer a few months earlier. But it was a fitting legacy, and gave hope to others. As a young man, he was exiled from the island as the result of a teenage prank. He got a job on the railways in Townsville, became a spokesperson for fellow laborers from the islands, and began mixing with trade unionists. Later, working as a university gardener, he began attending seminars and reading history and anthropology – especially what white 'experts' had written about his people. He made a key speech at a land rights conference in 1981, and a lawyer suggested bringing a test case. Eddie was chosen to lead the islanders in their action. However, not all indigenous activists call him a hero. Some say the court victory is already tarnished, and see the Mabo Decision as the latest confidence trick to be pulled on black Australians to further deny them land rights. ∎

See Gary Foley's essay 'Native title is NOT Land Rights' at
www.kooriweb.org/foley/essays/essay_2.html

cell lines are all being targeted by patent-hunters. Biopiracy has involved extracting the human genes of aboriginal communities that may be useful to science.

The industrialized world, led by the US, is trying to patent increasing numbers of plants and other living things, and it is pushing the South to set up systems for protecting intellectual property rights (IPR) on all inventions. Since the World Trade Organization (WTO) adopted the Agreement on Trade Related Aspects of Intellectual Property Rights (TRIPS), the developing countries have until 2005 to incorporate the granting of patents on inventions into national law. Part of the trouble with TRIPS is that it fails to protect the genetic resources of the South while allowing genetically modified (GM) materials to be patented. Who controls the GM process? The North, of course.[11] Indigenous peoples and most developing countries hope to tip the balance of control the other way through the Intergovernmental Committee on Intellectual Property and Genetic Resources, Traditional Knowledge and Folklore (IC). It is hoped that the IC will become a norm-setting body that

---

Folk hero: Louis Riel, Canada

Louis Riel was a Métis (indigenous person of mixed ancestry) who led the only armed resistance ever against the state in the Canadian North-West. Born in 1844 in the Red River Settlement in what is now Manitoba, he began training as a priest and then as a lawyer, but never completed either. He tried to set up an independent Métis state, after heading a provisional government from 1869-70. His involvement in the execution of Thomas Scott, one of a group sent to overthrow the rebels, led to his exile from Canada. While in exile he spent some time in an asylum, and came to believe he had a religious mission to lead the Métis people. In 1885, the Métis again declared a breakaway government. Riel led a short-lived armed rebellion that year, but was forced to surrender to Canadian forces. He was put on trial for treason, rejecting attempts by his lawyer to find him not guilty by reason of insanity. The jury found him guilty but recommended mercy. Judge Richardson had other ideas, and sentenced him to death. He was hanged in November 1885, which caused outrage across Quebec. ∎

Folk hero: Dame Whina Cooper, Aotearoa/New Zealand

Whina Cooper (1895-1994) was known as *Whaea o Te Motu*, or Mother of the Nation. Daughter of a chief of the Te Rarawa (*iwi*), Whina was just 18 when she won her first battle on behalf of Maori people by frustrating a *Pakeha* (the Maori word for European) farmer who was claiming land belonging to her people. She first became widely known when, at the age of 80, she led the 1975 Maori Land March on parliament, but she had already spent years working for the betterment of her people. A mother of six, she trained as a teacher but worked, among other things, as a postmistress, storekeeper and farmer. Besides fighting for Maori land rights she founded the Maori Women's Welfare League (*Te Ropu Wahine Maori Toko I te Ora*), set up to deal with issues such as health, housing, urbanization and loss of values experienced by young Maori. Some criticized Whina for accepting the title Dame of the British Empire. But she said at the time: 'If I accept this decoration I have more power to fight for all the Maori people against the government.' ∎

develops a binding legal system for protecting all these types of knowledge and resources.[12]

Here is one example, from Aotearoa/New Zealand, of an attempt to stem the tide of theft. The Wai262 Claim to Indigenous Flora and Fauna and Cultural and Intellectual Heritage Rights and Obligations was filed in 1991 with the Waitangi Tribunal. Hearings began in 1997, and are still going on. The claim was brought by Maori concerned about the increasing loss of native plants and animals. It is founded upon the rights guaranteed in Article 2 of the Treaty of Waitangi, quoted earlier (see **Trick or treaty?** p 98). It is about seeking recognition that *tino rangatiratanga* (the closest word to sovereignty in Maori language) was never given away by Maori, who still have a right to exercise full chiefly authority. The claim includes Maori demands to exercise rights over indigenous flora and fauna, to make decisions about the conservation and control of natural resources, and to take part in and benefit from technological advances to do with breeding, genetic manipulation and other processes connected with the use of fauna and flora.

Maori barrister Maui Solomon represents some of

Folk hero: Mama Yosepha, West Papua

In April 2002, Mama Yosepha Alomang, a leader of the Amungme people, was among eight people to win the Goldman Environmental Prize – the world's most prestigious environmental award. She won it for organizing resistance to gold mining that has devastated local rainforests. For more than 20 years she has led her community in the fight against Freeport, the company behind the world's largest gold mining operation. In 1994 Mama Yosepha was arrested by the Indonesian army during a clampdown aimed at protecting Freeport's interests. She was held and tortured for six weeks, and accused of giving food to resistance fighters. When they heard she was about to win the Goldman prize, Freeport (based in New Orleans, US) reportedly tried to bribe her by offering a big grant to the women's organization she founded – Hamak, the Foundation for Human Rights and Against Violence. This backfired spectacularly. Mama Yosepha has often attacked Freeport for trying to 'buy off' corrupt tribal leaders and the military. ■

Reproduced with the permission of TAPOL, the Indonesia Human Rights Campaign. www.tapol.gn.apc.org

---

the claimants. He says: 'Maori regard the genetic modification of flora and fauna as the interference or tampering with their *whakapapa* (geneology). Modifying or mixing the genes of the same or different species is analogous to genetic experiments on one's own family members. Whilst this may be regarded by some as emotional blackmail or 'over the top' emotionalism, the issue really boils down to one of respect.' The claim highlights the differences between two opposing world views: one that sees human beings as part of and not dominant over fauna and flora, and one that sees the natural world as ripe for exploitation and domination. In the Maori view, humans are obliged to respect the *mauri* or central life force of every living thing. People's rights to use natural things are balanced by obligations. Maori are not against development, says Maui Solomon. But they do insist that the Government, local authorities and commercial companies stop to consider the issues from their cultural perspective.[13]

Resistance will also feature in the next chapter, but in a different form: in music. Songs of freedom and struggle have long fired and inspired indigenous movements. Some have also become popular beyond the indigenous world, and entered the mainstream.

1 Peter Matthiessen, *In the Spirit of Crazy Horse*, (London 1992). **2** With thanks to Charles Swaisland for this information. **3** Taken partly from Andrew Gray, *Indigenous Rights and Development: Self-determination in an Amazonian community*, (Berghahn Books 1996), pp9-15. For a brief history of UN relations with indigenous peoples, see UNHCHR Fact Sheet No 9 (Rev. 1) viewable at www.unhchr.ch/html/menu6/2/fs9.htm **4** This uses information supplied by Lyndon Ormond Parker, and also draws on Jane Parker, 'Bones of contention', *The Guardian*, 9 July 2002. Also see the website of the European Network for Indigenous Australian Rights (ENIAR): www.eniar.org **5** There is more about the Ogiek campaign and their history on the website www.ogiek.org **6** From Amnesty International report on Colombia, AI Index AMR 23/43/94. **7** The quote is from Michael Howard, 'Iraq's Kurds assess risk of backing the US', *The Guardian*, 18 July 2002. Other information from Owen Bowcott, 'Homeless and friendless', *The Guardian*, 19 July 2002 (viewable on the web at Guardian Unlimited). **8** Draws on an article by Cameron Forbes in *New Internationalist* No 128, October 1983, updated from other sources. **9** See Larry Leventhal, 'Wounded Knee and the 1868 Treaty', *News from Indian Country*, May 1998, viewable at www.dickshovel.com/lsa12.html **10** An edited version of Gary Foley's account of the Aboriginal Embassy, used with his permission. **11** From Robert Ali Brac de la Perriere and Franck Seuret, *Brave New Seeds*, (Zed Books 2000). **12** For more information, see www.iwgia.org; articles on genetic resources and traditional knowledge on the website of the World Intellectual Property Organization, www.wipo.org, and in *Cultural Survival Quarterly*: www.culturalsurvival.org/quarterly **13** From 'Intellectual Property Rights and Indigenous Peoples' Rights and Obligations' by Maui Solomon, viewable at www.inmotionmagazine.com/ra01/ms2.html Additional information supplied direct by the author. The claim is expected to be completed in 2003.

6 Music and magic

Music is at the heart of indigenous culture... With other arts, it has helped shape global art forms... Indigenous musicians have enriched World Music, collaborating with others to create highly popular fusions... Songs of resistance drive and inspire rebel movements... and shamans use music and trance dance to work their magic and healing on the world.

MUSIC IS THE FOOD OF LIFE for indigenous communities. It is a vital form of communication, and marks the rites of passage from birth to death. Song is a vehicle for oral history and epic poems that tell of great sorrows, triumphs and other important events in the life of the community. It is used to praise as well as to curse. It appeals to the gods and ancestors, asking for their help in bringing rain and fertility. It inspires the warriors to rout their enemies, and young men and women to woo and win their loved ones. Subversive songs have played a massive role in resistance, when other forms of expression were banned or suppressed.

Some traditional forms

Music and singing are very much part of everyday life, as well as ceremonial occasions. They often accompany story telling, as elders gather round the fire with the younger generation after the day's labor is done. Songs and poetry embody philosophy, beliefs and values. They tell a people's history orally, which is vital in societies where not everyone is literate. They keep threatened languages alive and vibrant. They may be sung by one person, or consist of phrases sung by different people in turn. Unlike Western norms, there is rarely a division between performer and audience. Other people present

> You, whose day it is, make it beautiful.
> *Nootka song, US.*

will sing the chorus, or in some cases urge the singer on by saying something like 'Yes it is true' at the end of every verse.

Instruments are fashioned from natural materials, or whatever is available. On sacred occasions the Mbuti of Central Africa play a special trumpet, ideally made from the *molimo* tree, though it can also be fashioned from a piece of metal drainpipe. The Baka 'Pygmies' also make instruments from forest materials, and spend hours every day playing them. The music ranges from simple wordless melodies and clapping and rhyme games for children to *likanos*, longer and more complicated tales about myths of origin. Baka instruments include a thin string bow called *limbindi*, and the *ieta* or bow harp. They also make music without instruments – women and children bathing in the river will slap and beat their hands in the water to make polyrhythmic sounds called *liquindi*, or water drumming.

Among Sami people of Lapland the only traditional instrument is the drum, though musicians now use others. The oval single-headed drum is used by shamans to induce trances, and also in divination. The drum dances of the Inuit are played by one or two people on a small oval drum with a wooden frame covered with a bear bladder; they strike the frame instead of the skin. Drums are also central to the music of the Adivasis, or tribal people of India. The Maria (a subgroup) perform a fantastic marriage dance in which boys dance in circles, masked like bisons, accompanied by big cylindrical drums, while the girls dance in a row, beating iron bell-sticks on the ground. In New Guinea, indigenous instruments include the *garamut* or wooden slit drum, which can be anything from one to twelve feet long. Besides making music, it is used to send long-distance signals over land and sea.

Hunters sing about the animals they depend upon. The Mekranoti people of the Amazon sing in a high falsetto as they return from the hunt. From a long way off, villagers can tell who has killed what by the songs they hear. The Mbuti dance before setting off on a hunt – they circle the camp, singing special hunting songs while clapping their hands and leaping about in imitation of the game animals they hope to catch. Hunting songs are broken up into separate notes, each note being sung by one hunter. The *molimo* religious festival is a highpoint in Mbuti life. The men sing songs of praise to the forest, and the *molimo* answers them. (Though referred to as 'the animal of the forest', the *molimo* is actually someone playing a trumpet.) The words are simple and few – often, the Mbuti just sing that 'the forest is good'. But the message is powerful: songs lure the 'animal' to the special *molimo* fire, where dancers swirl in ecstasy through the flames.

Stock-keepers sing to their animals, praising their qualities as if singing about a lover. Praise songs also record warrior exploits, love affairs, great leaders and prophets. Prayer songs address the gods and bless the house, family and animals. Some societies, such as the Maasai, have no instruments besides the human voice, though kudu horns are blown to announce people's arrival at ceremonies such as *eunoto* (where junior warriors upgrade to senior). Australian Aboriginal people learn songs and chants as part of their initiation into adulthood. Each new generation must sing the landscape into being, just as the Dreamtime ancestors did. The traditional music of the Maori, meanwhile, is sung in a way that lies somewhere between speech and song – a style called heightened speech. A leader calls out the main words in a raised pitch and a chorus responds. The rhythm is kept going by vocal sounds and body percussions such as feet stamping, hand clapping and thigh slapping. Maori believe they cannot break the continuity of a song: that invites death or disaster. Chants such as the *patere* often tell the history of the group or describe someone's family tree. Such chants are common right across Oceania, for a person's place in society is very much linked to their family roots.

Music of resistance

From folk music to reggae, the sound of resistance rings out around the world, giving a voice to the oppressed. Rebel music tells alternative stories that challenge the dominant version of events. It records the struggle, and lionizes the heroes of struggle. Some indigenous musicians have even died for their beliefs, and what they represented as music makers. That was the fate of Arnold Ap from West Papua, who founded Mambesak in 1978. The band played songs of freedom, local radio stations loved them, and Mambesak could be heard on battery-powered boom-boxes in the most remote villages. But this was all too much for the government. The Indonesian authorities decided to take action before Ap's renown as a cultural icon got out of hand. The élite military task force, Kopassus, took him into custody in November 1983. He was held without charge for 66 days, then taken by prison guards to a beach where he was shot dead. The authorities claimed he had been trying to escape from prison. Now a new band, Black Paradise, is doing cover versions of Mambesak's songs of freedom. You cannot keep a good rebel song down.[1]

The struggle of the Saharawis of the Western Sahara is one of the most protracted independence struggles today. A whole generation has grown up in exile in squalid camps in Algeria, ever since Morocco invaded the Western Sahara in 1973. The outside world has shown little concern. Now ears are pricking up as the sound of Polisario Front resistance bursts out of the camps to reach a wider audience, thanks largely to Manuel Dominguez of the Spanish record label NubeNegra, who visited the camps in 1997 to record music at a festival. An important function of music in the camps is to safeguard and preserve Saharawi culture in the face of persecution. Says Dominguez of the extraordinary women's chants he recorded: 'They convey the emotional build-up of years and years of suffering.'[2]

The Kurds have long used music to keep the fire of cultural identity, and their ambitions for nationhood, burning. For centuries, it has been an important oral vehicle for poetry and history, and connected a scattered people. Kurdish language and literature have been suppressed by ruling regimes in the region. Musicians have been jailed and fled into exile. Until recently, all songs in Kurdish were banned in Turkey and both musicians and listeners were threatened with jail, torture and even death. Everything they sing has to be memorized and passed on orally, often through epic songs. Sivan Perwer is the most popular Kurdish singer today. Known as 'the voice of the Kurdish people', he sings about their longing to be free from persecution. He has been in exile from Turkish Kurdistan for more than 20 years.

On the other side of the world, the story of the late Vincent Lingiari and the fight for Gurindji country has been told in an epic song (see below) by two of Australia's leading songwriters. The words speak for themselves, but it is worth saying something more about this landmark event – the 1966 Gurindji walk-off. The Aboriginal Gurindji community was tired of seeing its land taken and its people used and abused as cheap labor by settlers. One of these exploiters was a Briton, Lord Vestey, who farmed Wave Hill station in the Northern Territory. On 23 August that year, Gurindji leader Vincent Lingiari led his people as well as members of the Ngarinman, Bilinara, Waripiri and Mudpara communities off the station. Vestey offered to raise their wages if they came back, but the strikers refused. They walked on to what they called their new promised land, Daguragu or Wattie Creek, where they held out for nine years. What began as a strike over Aboriginal cattle workers' wages and conditions became something much bigger – the fight to get their land back. Support for the cause came from right across Australia. Victory was a long time coming, but come it did. There has been an annual re-enactment of the walk-off ever since.

From Little Things Big Things Grow

Gather round people let me tell you a story
An eight year-long story of power and pride
British Lord Vestey and Vincent Lingiari
Were opposite men on opposite sides
Vestey was fat with money and muscle
Beef was his business, broad was his door
Vincent was lean and spoke very little
He had no bank balance, hard dirt was his floor...
Gurindji were working for nothing but rations
Where once they had gathered the wealth of the land
Daily the pressure got tighter and tighter
Gurindji decided they must make a stand
They picked up their swags and started off walking
At Wattie Creek they sat themselves down...
Eight years went by, eight long years of waiting
Till one day a tall stranger appeared in the land
And he came with lawyers and he came with great ceremony
And through Vincent's fingers poured a handful of sand
From little things big things grow
From little things big things grow...[3]

Indigenous contributions to World Music

World Music combines the oldest and newest musical forms on earth, from age-old traditions to the latest contemporary fusions. In the last five years, it has exploded into the most exciting and eclectic musical marketplace around. Festivals like WOMAD (which has just celebrated its 20th birthday) have brought World Music center stage. The movement, if it can be called that, has done more than anything else to bring indigenous music and languages to a wider audience. Though purists may abhor fusions, World Music is all about mixing, mingling and borrowing. Spiritual sounds jostle with the music of protest, rap or celebration. Western musicians working with colleagues from the South, in bands like Afro-Celt Sound System or the collaborations between 'Britpop' star Damon Albarn and Malian musicians, or Ry Cooder and Cuban players, have come up with fresh and original combinations to thrill the ear and move the feet. In fact, World Music makes nonsense of some of the arguments around guarding intellectual property – because music has no bounds and musicians have always borrowed from each other. Music is essentially fluid and derivative. If done with respect, musical borrowing brings people together and furthers our understanding of different cultures and histories. Respect must include giving indigenous musicians a fair share of the royalties on collaborative albums.

Many of these musicians create fusions that bridge cultures. They include people who are not themselves indigenous but draw on indigenous musical traditions, as seen below.

Yothu Yindi (meaning 'Mother Child') combine traditional Aboriginal music with modern Western instrumentation. Made up of Aboriginal and non-Aboriginal musicians, this wildly successful Australian band has brought the sound of the outback to the world, as well as promoting the struggle for Aboriginal rights. They aim to unite Australians and all other peoples of the world in peace. Lead singer Mandawuy Wunupingu was Australian of the Year in 1992, and he and fellow band member Witiyana Marika are sons of leaders of the Gumatj and Rirratjingu clans in Northeast Arnhem land, who took part in the Aboriginal land rights movement in the 1960s. Yothu Yindi's music also addresses social injustice and land rights issues, though running through it is the theme of reconciliation between black and white.

Zap Mama are an all-woman Belgian-African band who incorporate 'Pygmy' sounds, yodeling and other African and European styles into their unique a capella sound. Congo-born lead singer Marie Daulne got to know 'Pygmy' culture as a child after her Belgian father was killed in a rebellion and her mother took the children into the forests for eight months where 'Pygmies' protected them. The music reflects a mélange of influences, punctuated with all kinds of strange sounds including squeals, laughs and grunts. Daulne sees herself as a kind of global *griotte*, bringing the spiritual powers of the ancestors to the business of healing through harmony.

Mari Boine and her band marry Sami musical traditions and shamanistic beats with modern instrumentation to make what has been called 'vibrant minimalism, rock stripped bare'. She belongs to the radical Nordic school that reworks jazz, rock and traditional music. Mari is influenced both by Christian hymns and traditional *joik*, the improvised singing of the Sami people, and sings in the North Sami language. The *joik* has no formal structure, and can wander about according to the singer's whim. It can be about a person, an animal, a place or whatever the singer fancies. Mari Boine and her band play with the texture and shape of notes, drawing on sounds from other traditions such as Indian, Arabic, Native American and South American.

Senegalese superstars **Youssou N'Dour** and **Baaba Maal** have charmed millions of fans worldwide with their daring mix of indigenous and modern forms. N'Dour was born a *gawlo* or Tukulor (a sub-group of the Fula people) *griot* on his mother's side. Maal's background is also nomadic Fulani, and he sings in their language, Pulaar. UK-based band **Baka Beyond** mixes Baka sounds from Cameroon with Scottish ballads and Gypsy fiddling. Malian star **Salif Keita** is inspired by the melodies of Maninka hunters, while fellow Malian **Ali Farka Touré** draws on Songhai and Tuareg musical traditions.

Shamanism

Anthropologists like to remind their students that shamanism, not prostitution, is the world's oldest profession. For centuries, it has been puzzled over and sometimes derided by everyone from skeptical anthropologists to scientists and priests. One French priest, after seeing shamans at work in Brazil, called them 'ministers of the devil'. Anthropologist Claude Lévi-Strauss likened them to psychoanalysts. Today, their knowledge is better understood and admired, and their healing powers are legendary.

Shamans, who can be male or female, mediate between human beings and the spirit world. They communicate with spirits and may be possessed by them. Their powers include divination, prophecy,

---

Low thunder on the drum...

Black Elk, an Oglala Sioux, told poet John G Neihardt his life story in the 1930s. It included this description of how, in 1882 when he was just 19, he summoned the spirits to make his first cure. The patient was a sick boy, who recovered.

'Everything was ready now, so I made low thunder on the drum, keeping time as I sent forth a voice. Four times I cried 'Hey-a-a-hey', drumming as I cried to the Spirit of the World, and while I was doing this I could feel the power coming through me from my feet up, and I knew that I could help the sick little boy.

I kept on sending a voice... saying: 'My Grandfather, Great Spirit, you are the only one and to no other can any one send voices. You have made everything, they say, and you have made it good and beautiful. The four quarters and the two roads crossing each other, you have made. Also you have set a power where the sun goes down. The two-leggeds on earth are in despair. For them, my Grandfather, I send a voice to you... In vision you have taken me to the center of the world and there you have shown me the power to make over... To you and to all your powers and to Mother Earth I send a voice for help.'

[He then sings 'to the source of all life'.]

'While I was singing this I could feel something queer all through my body, something that made me want to cry for all unhappy things, and there were tears on my face. Now I walked to the quarter of the west, where I lit the pipe, offered it to the powers, and, after I had taken a whiff of smoke, I passed it around. When I looked at the sick little boy again, he smiled at me, and I could feel that the power was getting stronger.' ■

John G Niehardt, *Black Elk Speaks: being the life story of a holy man of the Oglala Sioux* (Morrow 1932).

healing, and charming animals in order to make them docile to hunt. They are fundamentally ambivalent; in order to cure people, they must also have the power to harm them. Some drink bitter substances like bark teas and vomit them up before they can make contact with the spirits. Others use hallucinogenic drugs. Powerful dreams convey many insights. Many shamans use drumming, singing and dancing to induce states of ecstasy and trance.

Here are two examples showing how shamanism is practiced in different parts of the world. There are many other forms it can take.

Siberian shamanism

This is probably the oldest form of spiritual healing in the world. It began in prehistoric times, and spread through China to the south and north. Chinese shamans invented and developed acupuncture and other healing practices. In the north, it spread over the Bering Strait into America, where shamans became the medicine people of the Native Americans. In Siberia, it nearly died out altogether under Stalin. Shamans were killed, or sent to the Gulag camps, and shamanism went underground for years.

Customarily, Siberian shamans deal with everything from illness to expelling bad spirits from people's homes and finding lost animals. They do not guarantee success in every case. They work by interceding between people and the spirit world. They heal by directing and sometimes deflecting spiritual energy, and usually go into a light trance (or sometimes a deep one) during a healing session.

They use many techniques, including the laying on of hands, and use drums as a vehicle to help them on their way. Patients talk of feeling energy moving round their bodies while they are being treated. Siberian shamanism is not an exact science or practice; each shaman has his or her own way of doing things. They also have their own specialties, such as healing children, or being good at extra-sensory perception.[4]

Shamanism among San people

From the evidence of rock paintings found right across southern Africa, archeologists claim a long history of the San's shamanic, transformative trance dance ritual. The dance is exceptional among indigenous shamanic rituals because the healers work indiscriminately with all who have gathered – including foreign researchers and tourists. This way of working is considered a distinctive example of the San's co-operative egalitarian behavior.

Typically – a hard word to use among people known for their flexibility – the dance consists of women sitting together in a tight semi-circle around a fire, singing a repetitive simple song and rhythmically clapping their hands. In the center a healer, or healers, usually men, dance in a shuffling and stamping manner. Using the energy of the women the healer seeks to tap into a healing energy, called *nǀom* in one of the San languages, Juǀ'hoansi. If all works well they feel a build-up of energy in their abdomen and chest as they dance. The process is painful and is often said to be like dying. If the energy builds up enough the healer can 'see' what is wrong with people. Having identified where the sickness is, the healer then rubs the afflicted area of the person's body. This draws the sickness into his own body; the healer must then expel the sickness out through the top of his head or the bottom of his neck.

Different San peoples describe what they do and see during 'trance' healing in different ways. General themes involve the healer climbing up a thread from his body to the home of god or the devil (not that the San call it this – generally, they do not believe in a fully evil being) where he must plead for the life of the sick person. Sometimes healers say they change into lions or ride away into the night on the backs of eland or other animals. When they change shape, healers are often described as undergoing transformation. Similarly the dance ritual is often regarded as a transformative process in which differences, sickness, problems and anger can be reconciled and life thereby remains a possibility in a testing social and physical environment.[5]

But not even the shamans can prevent some of the major challenges facing indigenous peoples. The final chapter looks at some of these challenges in the light of 'development' and tries to offer some conclusions.

1 Adapted from Eben Kirksey, 'Playing up the primitive', *New Internationalist* No 344, and personal communication. **2** The quote is from *The Rough Guide to World Music* Vol 1, p 565. Much of this section draws, with the publishers' permission, from the two-volume *Rough Guide to World Music*, edited by Simon Broughton, Mark Ellingham and Richard Trillo (Rough Guides 2000). **3** Edit of *From Little Things Big Things Grow* by Paul Kelly and Kev Carmody. Information taken from www.lingiari.startyourweb.com **4** With thanks to Ken Hyder, journalist, musician and shaman, for supplying this information. **5** Thanks to Chris Low for writing this contribution.

7 Development, justice and future challenges

Development schemes aimed at helping indigenous peoples have often done more harm than good... Communities now demand to take control of their own development and speak for themselves... What are the lessons of development intervention and how can social justice be achieved?

'Don't mistake us. We are not a backward-looking people, Like others we want development and we want to improve our lives and the lives of the next generations... But we want to control this development in our land and over our lives. And we demand a share both in decision-making and in the benefits of development.'

Unnamed tribal person, the Philippines.

OVER THE CENTURIES, indigenous peoples have suffered a great deal at the hands of those who sought to 'develop' them. Colonizers, missionaries, anthropologists, governments and aid agencies – they have all had a go. Some had the best will in the world, some had the worst. Either way, it was usually misplaced because indigenous peoples did not tend to ask for it. It was (and still is) often driven by racism and the belief that indigenous peoples were backward, and therefore obstacles to national development.

Development: good or bad?

Now they demand the right to develop on their own terms and at their own pace. Some groups have created a model for change that builds on their traditional self-reliance. Some have been able to develop and strengthen their negotiating power with the state, and with outsiders who try to exploit them. These models are useful for others to follow. Sensitive governments, aid agencies and human rights organizations would do well to listen and learn. Equally, though indigenous peoples have the right to refuse contact, there are strong arguments for their being open to forging useful alliances with outside organizations, and lobbying alongside others. For some say it is the 'separateness' of indigenous peoples that has placed them so much at risk, together with their uneasy relationship with national society. Those who argue that they are best left that way – remote, untouched and untainted by the modern world – may be condemning them to extinction. Isolation can deprive indigenous peoples of the skills and knowledge they need to defend themselves; otherwise they risk seeing more of their rights and land eroded. Also, seeking legal redress for injustice at courts in the Western world may lead to better outcomes: the compensation is bigger, there is less likelihood of local bigwigs and corrupt politicians

intervening, and the media coverage is sure to raise awareness of your story all around the world.[1] This is one of the potential payoffs of North-South alliances, on this and other social justice issues. On the other hand, indigenous peoples who choose to remain isolated have every right to do so, and must have their land and other rights respected regardless of their relationship with wider society and the state.

Nonetheless, most people would agree that the modern world cannot be kept at bay indefinitely. The

> 'The Government talks about development. Let it help us with water, then leave us to our own place. We can think for ourselves; we can think about what we need.'
> *Mogetse Kaboikanyo, Kgalagadi man, Botswana. Quoted in Survival appeal on behalf of the San, August 2002. Kaboikanyo, who was in his 50s, died shortly after being evicted by the Botswana Government from the Central Kalahari Game Reserve.*
>
> 'I hope we can get to the point where we don't have to be frozen images of the past.'
> *Sandra Sunrising Osawa, Makah filmmaker, US.*

challenge for development workers and indigenous groups is 'how to exploit the useful features of modern society without alienation and suffering'.[2] This is what two young San people, one from South Africa and the other from Namibia, have to say about the kind of development the San want, which seeks to strike a balance between upholding 'traditional' culture while using what the outside world can offer. Both of them are involved with the Working Group of Indigenous Minorities in Southern Africa (WIMSA, see end of chapter 4), established by the San in 1996 as an umbrella organization to enable their widely scattered communities to communicate with each other and to represent the San nationally and internationally.

Example: San want development at their own pace

'WIMSA believes that San communities themselves should find ways to be involved in development. Rather than wait for governments to act, they should initiate self-development programs - with children, youth, parents and elders, or all age groups together so the rich culture and traditions are imparted to new generations. We need the freedom to implement our self-development projects at our own pace. Experience has taught us to keep projects simple so they are sustainable. We now see San groups in Namibia, Botswana and South Africa setting up income-generating projects such as tourist campsites and craft shops, and establishing San kindergartens where community members tell traditional stories and teach tracking skills and traditional games.

As for assistance from outside, we need to build our capacity, learn how to organize ourselves and make longer-term plans. We need assistance with training, especially in bookkeeping, computer operating, marketing, catering, agriculture, tourism and entrepreneurship. We hope governments and NGOs will assist us with training. We also hope for opportunities to participate in meetings that enable us to network with other indigenous groups. We need schools where young children are taught in their mother tongue, and human rights and HIV/AIDS awareness programs in our own languages. Most of all we need land. Our ancestral lands were all lost to colonial powers and dominant ethnic groups. Without land we have no culture, no traditions, no livelihood.'[3]

'Bad development' globally has included:
• forced assimilation of indigenous peoples into national society
• forced urbanization and resettlement schemes
• forced removals and relocation
• national development projects created at indigenous peoples' expense, for example by building highways and hydroelectric projects, or allowing such things as mining, oilfields and commercial hunting on indigenous land
• promoting strong ethnic groups over weaker ones
• supporting men and ignoring women
• ignoring children's rights
• giving control of wildlife and 'conservation' to Western-driven bodies
• introducing inappropriate technology
• forcing religious, political or other alien ideologies upon people.

Flawed development schemes include both top-down mega-projects (those imposed from on high) and smaller community projects. What indigenous peoples want is bottom-up alternatives (those arising from the grassroots) to the discredited top-down models, that recognize their human rights, particularly their collective rights to land, natural resources and a healthy environment of their choosing. Indigenous peoples also want empowerment in the form of information, pros and cons, so that they are able to make informed decisions.

When 'bad development' goes wrong, indigenous peoples and the environment pay dearly. Some ill-thought out schemes have wrecked the latter. Many indigenous territories contain high levels of biological diversity, and provide vital water catchment functions for large geographic regions. When this ecosystem is disrupted, it not only affects indigenous communities but wider non-indigenous irrigation and farming systems that rely upon its water supplies and other resources. Some development schemes have also upset relationships between men and women, usually at the expense of women – by taking away women's land and resource rights and undermining their role as producers and traders. Others have stoked up tensions and rivalries between indigenous and other communities, leading to bloodshed. Food aid has created dependency. Concentrating wells, bore-holes, schools, churches and clinics in one place has led to bloated townships where newly sedentarized nomads scrap over meager resources – and women despair because their unemployed men have taken to drink.

So what should responsible governments, NGOs and other development actors do? They must beware of imposing any ideology, however worthy. An intervention that involves political action can backfire, triggering reprisals for the indigenous group concerned. Where several NGOs compete for influence over a particular

> 'Stop all logging activities... Give back to us what is properly ours. Save our lives, have respect for our culture.'
> *1987 declaration by the Penan people of Borneo.*

> 'I believe in our fight for sovereignty and I believe if we are to accept anything less then we will be selling ourselves short.'
> *Darlene Mansell, Aboriginal woman, Australia.*

indigenous group, as has happened in the Amazon, there can be dire effects for the supposed beneficiaries. Other pitfalls to avoid include paternalism, ethnocentric attitudes, ignoring indigenous skills and indigenous knowledge, giving hand-outs, only supporting indigenous groups who are well-organized and can help themselves (because that is easier), using dubious power brokers, and being in too much of a hurry. Outside agencies must avoid top-down strategies.

'Good development' includes providing resources for the self-management of projects, enabling indigenous groups to gain political and legal representation and secure land and resource rights. Encouraging consensus, and urging people to transcend traditional divisions in order to present a united front. Meeting real needs. Helping to restore confidence, and allowing plenty of time. Building consultation and

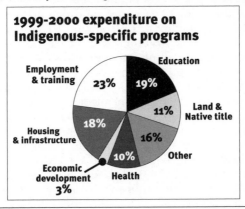

Money matters

Australian government spending on indigenous-specific programs for housing, health and so on. In 1999-2000 the Government allocated Aus$ 2,239 million (US$ 1,253 million) compared with Aus$ 1,984 million (US$ 1,111 million) in the previous year. Increased spending is welcome but may not be enough to overcome the stark inequalities.

1999-2000 expenditure on Indigenous-specific programs

- Education 19%
- Land & Native title 11%
- Other 16%
- Health 10%
- Economic development 3%
- Housing & infrastructure 18%
- Employment & training 23%

www.dfat.gov.au

participation into all development work. Showing respect. Identifying priorities instead of trying to solve all problems at once. Supporting women's and children's rights and development. Providing mobile services for nomads (clinics, schools, 'barefoot doctors' and vets). Providing literacy, numeracy, management, rights and advocacy training. Three examples of good practice are the training that Anti-Slavery, Franciscans International and Trócaire did for partner organizations on how to use the UN's International Labour Organization (ILO) mechanisms to combat trafficking and bonded labor.[4] In South America, First Peoples Worldwide is working with local partners on a new project called 'Speaking Up', which aims to improve the capacity of indigenous communities to address the threats they face from the extractive resource industry. In a US-Africa collaboration, Africans are being trained to use indigenous knowledge for conflict resolution/management on their continent.[5] There are many others.

Bad development is not, of course, only caused by NGOs. The World Bank, state governments and private corporations have run riot over indigenous territories with their dams, roads, mines, logging, oil and gas extraction and other schemes – often carried out in the name of 'progress' and national development. For example, the US company PT Freeport has devastated the central highlands of West Papua with its gold and copper mining operations (see **Folk hero** Mama Yosepha p 106). It has even cut the top off one mountain, believed by the indigenous Amungme people to be the sacred head of their mother; the Amungme see Freeport now dipping into her heart. Freeport plans to increase its dumping of untreated tailings into the Aghawaghon River system to 285,000 tons daily – the equivalent of a ten-ton truckload every three seconds. Indigenous people have not only seen their environment trashed, but have also died and suffered at the hands of the Indonesian military which has provided 'security' for Freeport throughout its 42-year presence in West Papua.[6]

Indigenous voices at the 'Earth Summit'

Many of these issues were raised by indigenous peoples' representatives who attended the World Summit on Sustainable Development (WSSD), held in Johannesburg in August 2002. They got a one-line statement about indigenous peoples' vital role in sustainable development included in the Summit's final declaration – a seemingly small but significant achievement. An international indigenous peoples' summit on the same subject was also held in Khoisan territory in Kimberley, South Africa, just before the WSSD. Out of this came the Kimberley Declaration, which sets out indigenous views of sustainable development while calling for key rights to be respected. For example: 'We have the right to determine and establish priorities and strategies for our self-development and for the use of our lands, territories and other resources.'[7]

At the WSSD, indigenous representatives drew up an Indigenous Peoples' Plan of Implementation on Sustainable Development. 'The plan', they said, 'reflects the heart and mind of Indigenous Peoples as traditional caretakers of Mother Earth who, for many millennia, have developed and refined our sustainable societies'. Their presence at this event, and the plan itself, possibly represented a defining moment for the indigenous movement on the world stage. Indigenous representatives were contributing to an international debate, offering a unique critique of local-global issues that is grounded in their own cultural experience as natural resource owners and managers. While in part driven by self-interest, and the need to seize the opportunity to raise public awareness of indigenous rights, they were simultaneously looking outward – and acting in partnership with hundreds of other, non-indigenous interest groups – in a way that they had not done quite so visibly and powerfully before. In some ways, the indigenous movement stole the show.

The 100-point plan is too long to reproduce here. But it covers 'cosmovision' and spirituality, self-determination and territory, treaties, children and youth, women, sacred sites, food security, indigenous knowledge and intellectual property rights, biodiversity, forests and protected areas, mining, energy, tourism, fisheries and marine resources, water, climate change, health, desertification, education, science, technology and communications, security and conflict resolution, sustainable livelihoods, corporate accountability, governance and human rights. Rights to self-determination, and the collective ownership, control and management of indigenous lands and natural resources, are central themes. Some other key points include:

• We demand that the concept of cultural damage be incorporated to impact assessments as part of the legal instruments which will safeguard our cultural integrity against energy mega-projects, mining, tourism, logging and other unsustainable activities (point 3)

• We reaffirm the rights of indigenous women and their vital role in human, cultural and environmental sustainability... We take deliberation steps to ensure that [they] participate in all levels of governance and leadership both locally, nationally and internationally (point 17)

• We commit ourselves to protect indigenous knowledge systems and the diversity of life within our territories which are collective resources... We will work against any Intellectual Property Rights (IPR) regime that attempts to assert patents, copyrights, or trademark monopolies for products, data or processes derived or originating from our knowledge (point 28)

• We will oppose biopiracy and the patenting of all life forms (point 36)

• We oppose and denounce the privatization of water (point 56)

• We urge the United States and all other countries

which have not done so, to ratify and implement the Kyoto Protocol (point 58).[8]

Landmark agreement

A new blueprint is the Partnership Agreement on Indigenous Rights and Sustainable Development between the Danish Government, Greenland Home Rule and indigenous peoples, also launched at the WSSD. This aims to ensure that indigenous peoples take part in sustainable development and are fully recognized in development policies in general. It is supported by Norway, Finland and the United Nations Development Program (UNDP).[9]

Example: breakthrough Cree agreement, Canada

Below, Romeo Saganash, lawyer and spokesman for the Cree Council of the Cree Nation talks about their agreement.

'It's hard to make dispossession of lands compatible with human rights, no matter how long ago it took place. Indigenous peoples can only survive and prosper if they can use their lands; that is fundamental.

In February 2002, a breakthrough agreement was signed between the Cree Nation and the Government of Quebec which could be the basis for a rights-based approach elsewhere in the world. They are the only government to recognize the mutually beneficial nature of an understanding with indigenous peoples based on cooperation, partnership and mutual respect. Before, development on our lands mostly benefited others. Land laws were based on the erroneous idea that indigenous people could not manage the land economically, which forced us into a position of dependency on the Government and a life on the edge of poverty. Now, the Cree will be responsible for their own development and economy, and will benefit directly from development. The agreement includes a new forestry regime that will involve consultation with the Cree, the cancellation of a controversial hydro-electric project on Cree land, more Cree involvement in mining that will lead to more jobs for Cree, and the establishment of a Cree

Development Corporation.

Unusually, this agreement is not based on damages but makes the Cree part of the official development process. This disturbs some people, including some Cree who have become used to the idea of indigenous peoples being opposed to governments and development. The Quebec Government and the Cree have bravely abandoned the old oppositional positions.' [10]

Voices and choices: indigenous peoples and aid

Mike Sansom of African Initiatives outlines some lessons and challenges (below). African Initiatives is a social justice organization that promotes the rights of all people fully to participate in the social, political and economic decisions that affect their lives at a community, national and international level. It supports communities and their organizations in Africa by providing resources, training, advice and advocacy.

'In a world where people often profess utopian ideals of egalitarianism and sharing natural resources for the common good, it is a sad irony that those communities which come nearest to attaining that dream are in danger of being wiped out.

All indigenous peoples have their own social structures and organization. Yet most non-governmental organizations (NGOs) encourage them to set up new organizations, which invariably represent Western hierarchical models, and subsequently fail. While NGOs proclaim cultural sensitivity, many seem to deny or ignore the legitimacy of traditional social, political and economic systems. NGOs also tend to claim that they are committed to participatory approaches to working with communities – yet they often miss or avoid the priority issues. The primary threat to indigenous peoples is the loss of their land, yet most

'We recognize that the fight is a long one and we cannot hope to win it alone. To win, to secure the future, we must join hands with like-minded people and create strength through unity.'
The Haudenosaunee Declaration of the Iroquois, US.

'I just want to wander in freedom in my country.'
Unnamed Tuareg woman, Burkina Faso.

> 'We will not accept any cosmetic solution short of total and complete national independence... East Timor will be free, independent and sovereign.'
> *Roque Rodriques of FRETILIN, the liberation movement of East Timor, in 1979.*

> 'We don't want power over white institutions; we want white institutions to disappear. *That's* revolution.'
> *Russell Means, Native American activist.*

development agencies continue to focus on service delivery.

Conservation is a major threat to indigenous peoples all over Africa. Hunter-gatherers face extinction, and have been banned from carrying bows and arrows while seeing their lands turned into commercial hunting blocks, which some conservationists regard as legitimate land use. To my knowledge no major NGO is challenging the methods and legitimacy of conservation organizations. The major conservation NGOs are actually strengthening government departments that promote this approach. If Shell Oil or a government were alienating people from vast tracts of land there would be an NGO outcry. One example is Serengeti National Park in Tanzania. Serengeti, the size of Northern Ireland, has been denied to pastoralists for over a generation. So why do the major development NGOs mimic the three monkeys – hear no evil, see no evil, speak no evil – when conservation bodies contribute to the marginalization and impoverishment of indigenous peoples, and in some cases threaten their very survival?

If they are to survive, indigenous peoples need security of land, appropriate education and self-representation. With these, they will be better equipped to determine their own destiny. Education will enable them to expand their world view, understand their place in the world and adapt their mode of production by acquiring new skills. If they choose to retain traditional modes such as pastoralism, it will be done from an informed and secure base. This should be the focus of development interventions; unfortunately, it is not. Northern development and rights organizations (some do make a distinction) are often disempowering, taking away the right of indigenous peoples to tell their own story and represent themselves. If the emphasis is on service delivery (funding

healthcare, education, water supplies and other basic services) this can unwittingly undermine local culture with zero or
negative impacts.

In our experience, taking land cases to court is rarely successful, puts resources and control in the hands of lawyers
and NGOs, and increases tension between governments and
indigenous peoples. Likewise high profile campaigns in the
North done 'on behalf of' indigenous peoples are not account-
able to affected communities, can have negative consequences
and reinforce the patronizing myth that indigenous peoples
cannot represent themselves.

Community advocacy

An alternative approach is community advocacy. This involves
recognizing and building on the legitimacy of indigenous peoples' social processes. Instead of doing advocacy 'on behalf of'
people, communities control their own representation.
Community advocacy also includes research, documentation
and, crucially, analysis of their situation. It is a social process
that starts at community level, and enables people to make
clear links between their micro-political situation and the macro
one. For example, providing a Tanzanian pastoralist organization with information on debt and structural adjustment
enabled them to analyze the forces and interests behind their
eviction from traditional lands in the name of conservation.

Northern NGOs have to be careful not to dominate the
debate around globalization, denying the space to indigenous
peoples in particular to develop their own critiques, analyses
of how they fit into the world and strategies for influencing it.
Strengthening the voices of marginalized peoples is the beginning of democratization and global justice. Community
advocacy gives a voice and choice to indigenous peoples and
has the potential to fundamentally challenge the inequities of
economic globalization.'

What lies ahead

Self-development and self-determination are the key
words. These drive the indigenous movement, and all
who wish to support it. The right to self-determination

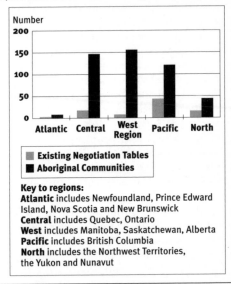

Self-government in Canada, 2001

Since 1984, self-government legislation has been enacted on behalf of the Cree and Naskapi bands of Quebec and the Sechelt of British Columbia. It has also been enacted on behalf of some of the Yukon First Nations. In April 2000 the Nisga'a Final Agreement came into force; it is the first modern land claim agreement explicitly to extend special protection to both land and self-government rights.

Number

Atlantic **Central** **West Region** **Pacific** **North**

- Existing Negotiation Tables
- Aboriginal Communities

Key to regions:
Atlantic includes Newfoundland, Prince Edward Island, Nova Scotia and New Brunswick
Central includes Quebec, Ontario
West includes Manitoba, Saskatchewan, Alberta
Pacific includes British Columbia
North includes the Northwest Territories, the Yukon and Nunavut

www.ainc-inac.gc.ca

is a fundamental principle of human rights law, and represents the individual and collective right of people (not simply governments) to freely determine their political status and pursue economic, social and cultural development. The principle is linked to the decolonization process that followed the UN Charter of 1945, in which self-determination featured strongly. Two important UN studies concluded that people have a right to self-determination if they have a history of independence or self-rule in an identifiable territory, a distinct culture, and a will and capability to regain self-government.[11] However, many indigenous peoples failed to gain from decolonization because it did not restore sovereignty or full governance. Very often, colonial powers relinquished control to one group of people in a contested territory, leaving other groups out in the cold. Colonization has even continued in some places; one example is Tibet, seized by China in 1949-50 and occupied ever since. The problem now is that the international community has largely ignored indigenous peoples' call for recognition of their right to self-determination, dismissing it as political rhetoric.[12]

Some communities are striving for complete territorial autonomy, self-government and recognition of sovereignty. Realistically, they are unlikely to achieve full sovereignty in today's world of nation states, and none have so far done so. Most indigenous peoples claim that they have never given up their sovereignty, and accuse nation states of violating it on a daily basis. Others may settle for running some of their own affairs, controlling local political institutions and revenues from such money-spinners as tourism and mining on their land. Either way, there are potential snags. Self-determination rarely guarantees indigenous peoples' complete freedom from oppression or full recognition of their rights. Self-interested leaders may feel it gives them the right to do what they like, at the expense of weaker sections of the community – such as women, youngsters or disabled people. Power may become concentrated in fewer hands, and some people may interpret self-management as the right to claim funds while denying accountability.

Unfortunately there have been cases of indigenous NGOs becoming dependent on handouts, and failing to account for these to their own communities. When there is big money to be had, indigenous leaders (and any other leaders for that matter) can sometimes become more oriented to international donors than their own people. There is also a danger of indigenous élites in multi-ethnic societies dominating the development agenda at the expense of other marginalized ethnic groups. By representing itself as indigenous, thereby making itself more eligible for donor funding, a group may aggrandize itself over others in the same area – driving a wedge between one community and its neighbors. These are uncomfortable truths, by no means universal, which should be aired and discussed nonetheless. How can such problems be overcome? There may be lessons to be learned from longer established social movements such as the women's movement, the environmental movement, gay rights, the American civil rights movement and Black Power. Though widely divergent in many ways, they faced similar challenges at certain points in their history around power imbalances, internal dissent and funding.

In the scramble for rights, and UN recognition, there is a danger of privileging one ethnic group over another, leading to jealousies, inequalities and trampled rights. Is it fair that Nuer people are considered to be indigenous, but not Kikuyu? Maasai, but not the Ndebele? The Indigenous Peoples of Africa Coordinating Committee (IPACC) suggests there is no contradiction: 'All Africans should enjoy full and equal rights. There are principles about collective rights in the UN Draft Declaration that could be usefully applied in Africa, beyond the claims of indigenous peoples. This does not negate the importance of using the UN process to challenge the systematic discrimination against peoples' aboriginal identities and their continued use of ancient territories, economic and cultural practices.' In Africa, it says, 'it is the maintenance of systematic inequality and marginalization that defines who is indigenous today'.[13]

But this remains a difficult issue. There is a tightrope to be walked between showing due reverence for marginalized peoples, ethnic reification (and the hardening of ethnic boundaries that goes with that) and acknowledging the genuine needs and

rights of particular communities. Indigenous and tribal peoples should remember that they are themselves
the product of colonial attempts to 'fix' ethnic identity. In fact, tribes and tribal identities are and were
always fluid. We need to keep a sense of perspective
and a good grasp of history.

Intellectual property rights are another minefield,
towards which indigenous peoples are rushing head-
long. They rightly want to stop exploitation and
biopiracy, and to gain a share of any profits. But perhaps they should beware of buying into the Western
obsession with money: has everything got a price
now? Must everything be commoditized and sold?
Knowledge exists to be shared by all – ordinary citizens, academics, writers, artists, musicians,
researchers, scientists and indigenous peoples. If one
takes the opposite view, this closes the door to schol-
arship and prevents mutually useful collaborations,
such as those described in chapters 3 and 6.
However, the Kimberley Declaration is unequivocal:
'Our traditional knowledge is not in the public
domain; it is collective, cultural and intellectual
property protected under our customary law.
Unauthorized use and misappropriation of traditional knowledge is theft.'

It now looks highly unlikely that the UN Draft
Declaration will be agreed and adopted before the
decade of indigenous peoples ends in 2004. A major
breakthrough is the new Permanent Forum on
Indigenous Issues, though some people have already
expressed cynicism. Rudolph C Rÿser, chair and exec-
utive director of the Center for World Indigenous
Studies has written: 'The Indigenous Peoples' Forum
is a hoax played upon indigenous peoples. The central question raised by advocates of the Forum is not
whether the Forum can actually represent specific
concerns and interests of indigenous nations or do
anything about those concerns – they want to know
whether they will personally be appointed to [it].'[14]

He pointed out that membership of the Forum will be determined by representatives of governments, not by indigenous peoples. In the last year, indigenous groups have worked hard to ensure that they would in fact control the nomination of the eight indigenous experts on the Forum. Indigenous peoples are also demanding that the Forum must have its own secretariat, staffed by indigenous persons, instead of coming under the UN's Economic and Social Council (ECOSOC). Rather than indulge in skepticism, let's give the Forum a chance to prove itself. Its chairperson, Ole Henrik Magga, welcomes it for enabling 'people who have been left out in the cold and dark to come into a warm well-lighted house to discuss things that mattered to them'.

Collectively, indigenous peoples are now a force to be reckoned with. They have scored major victories in the last 20 years. They have become highly visible and vocal, especially in the global justice/anti-globalization movement where they have raised key questions about the social and ecological crisis that threatens the world. It was they who first alerted us all to our unsustainable relationship with 'Mother Earth' – and they were right. The next ten years will prove crucial as they fight for rights, reparations and recognition. The 21st century is a new age of discovery, as those who were first 'discovered' explore and exercise their many strengths, and attempt to redress past wrongs.

The mood is summed up by a group of anti-nuclear activists, at whose core are Western Shoshone people, who declared on the eve of a protest at the US Government's Nevada test site in Native American territory: *'Together... we will wise up, rise up, honor and resist'*.[15]

1 For example, see the 2002 Maasai legal action in London (mentioned in chapter 5). Also, a landmark human rights lawsuit against Unocal Corp. is set to go to trial in the US, alleging human rights abuses committed by the Burmese army on behalf of Unocal's Yadana Pipeline project in southern Burma. It is the first case in US history in which a corporation is to stand trial for human rights abuses committed abroad. See www.earthrights.org **2** From Beauclerk and Narby with Townsend, *Indigenous Peoples: a field-guide*. The first part of this chapter draws upon this manual. **3** Written for this book by Victoria Geingos and Tommy A Busakhwe, members of the Hai ‖om and Khomani San groups respectively. **4** The workshop drew on a booklet that Anti-Slavery and the Minority Rights Group produced for the ILO, see Chandra Roy and Mike Kaye, 'The International Labour Organization: A Handbook for Minorities and Indigenous Peoples' (2002). This explains the workings of the ILO, how it can help defend and promote people's rights, and how indigenous and minority groups can work with it. **5** See *Indigenous Knowledge and Development Monitor* Vol 3, Issue 3 (December 1995), p 27. **6** See www.moles.org/ProjectUnderground/mother-lode/freeport/tenrisks.html **7** For the full text, see www.iwgia.org **8** These are edited excerpts. For the full transcript, see for example www.tebtebba.org **9** For the full text, see www.iwgia.org **10** From a talk given in Oxford, UK, October 2002. For more information, visit www.gcc.ca **11** Studies by H Gros Espiel and A Critescu, both 1980. See Parker, below. **12** From Karen Parker, 'Understanding Self-Determination: The Basics', a presentation to the First International Conference on the Right to Self-Determination, UN, Geneva, August 2000, viewable at www.webcom.com/hrin/parker/self-det.html **13** From 'Who are indigenous Africans?' at www.firstpeoples.org **14** From *Fourth World Eye*, the online newsletter for the Center for World Indigenous Studies, No 11, February 2001. **15** The Action for Nuclear Abolition and the Shundahai Network, protest at Nevada test site 5-12 October 2002, cited on www.firstpeoples.org

CONTACTS

International

Amnesty International
1 Easton Street, London WC1X 8DJ, UK
Tel +44 (0) 20 7413 5500
Fax +44 (0) 20 7956 1157
email: amnesty@gn.apc.org
website: www.amnesty-international.org

Anti-Slavery International
Thomas Clarkson House,
The Stableyard Broomgrove Road,
London SW9 9TL, UK
Tel +44 (0) 20 7501 8920
Fax +44 (0) 20 7738 4110
email: info@anti-slavery.org
website: www.antislavery.org

Center for World Indigenous Studies (CWIS)
PMB 214
1001 Cooper Point Road SW 140,
Olympia, Washington 98502-1107, US
Tel +1 (360) 754 1990
Fax +1 (253) 276 0084
email: usaoffice@cwis.org
website: www.cwis.org

Cultural Survival
215 Prospect Street, Cambridge,
MA 02139, US
Tel +1 (617) 441 5400
Fax +1 (617) 441 5417
email: csinc@cs.org
website: www.culturalsurvival.org

First Peoples Worldwide
The Stores Building, 11917 Main Street,
Fredericksburg, VA 22498, US
Tel +1 (540) 371 5615
Fax +1 (540) 371 3505
email: infofpw@firstnations.org
website: www.firstpeoples.org

International Indian Treaty Council (IITC)
Tel +1 (415) 641 4482
Fax +1 (415) 641 1298
email: iitc@igc.apc.org
website: www.treatycouncil.org

International Labour Organization
(Project for Indigenous and Tribal
Peoples Equality and Employment
Branch)
4 Route des Morillons
CH-1211 Geneva-22, Switzerland
Tel +41 22 799 7115
Fax +41 22 798 6344
email: egalite@ilo.org
website: www.ilo.org

International Work Group for Indigenous Affairs (IWGIA)
Classensgade 11E
DK-2100 Copenhagen, Denmark
Tel +45 35 27 0500
Fax +45 35 27 0507
email: iwgia@iwgia.org
website: www.iwgia.org

Minority Rights Group International (MRG)
379 Brixton Road, London SW9 7DE, UK
Tel +44 (0) 20 7978 9498
Fax +44 (0) 20 7738 6265
email: minority.rights@mrg.org
website: www.minorityrights.org

Survival International
6 Charterhouse Buildings
London EC1M 7ET
Tel +44 (0) 20 7687 8700
Fax +44 (0) 20 7687 8701
email: info@survival-international.org
website: www.survival-international.org

Africa

First Peoples of the Kalahari
PO Box 173, Ghanzi, Botswana
Tel/fax +267 596101
email: fpk@info.bw

Indigenous Peoples of Africa Co-ordinating Committee (IPACC)
PO Box 106, Rondebosch 7725,
South Africa
Tel/fax: +27 (0) 21 686 0193
email: ipacc@iafrica.org.za
website: www.ipacc.org.za

South African San Institute (SASI)
PO Box 12995, Mowbray 7705,
Cape Town, South Africa
Tel +27 21 686 0795
Fax +27 21 685 4223
email: sasi@iafrica.com
website: www.san.org.za

Working Group of Indigenous Minorities in Southern Africa (WIMSA)
PO Box 80733, Windhoek, Namibia
Tel +264 61 244909
Fax +264 61 272806
email: wimsareg@iafrica.com.na
website: www.san.org.za

Also **WIMSA Botswana**:
c/o Mathambo Ngakaeaja
PO Box 219, Ghanzi, Botswana
Tel +267 6597520
email: wimsa@info.bw

Contacts

Australia

Aboriginal peoples' website
www.kooriweb.org
(for Gary Foley's writings on history, add /foley)
www.whoseland.com
(interactive land rights site with world-wide focus)

Canada

Assembly of First Nations
One Nicholas Street, Suite #1002,
Ottawa ON K1N 7B7
Tel +1 (613) 241 6789
Fax +1 (613) 241 5808
website: www.afn.ca/

Métis Resource Centre
506-63 Albert Street, Winnipeg,
Manitoba R3B 1G4
Tel +1 (204) 956 7767
Fax +1 (204) 956 7765
website:
www.metisresourcecentre.mb.ca/mrc/index.htm

Indigenous Peoples Biodiversity Information Network (IBIN)
355 Yellowhead Highway,
Kamloops, BC V2H 1H1
Tel +1 (250) 828 9761
Fax +1 (250) 828 9787
website: www.ibin.org

Inuit Tapiriit Kanatami
170 Laurier Avenue West,
Suite 510, Ottawa, Ontario
K1P 5V5
(613) 238-8181
website: www.itk.ca/

And some indigenous media...

Aboriginal Peoples Television Network
website: www.aptn.ca/

Turtle Island News
website: www.turtleislandnews.on.ca

Europe

The European Network for Indigenous Australian Rights (ENIAR)
www.eniar.org

UK

African Initiatives
Brunswick Court, Brunswick Square,
Bristol BS2 8PE
Tel +44 (0) 1179 150001
email: info@african-initiatives.org.uk
website: www.african-initiatives.org.uk

The Dana Declaration on Mobile Peoples and Conservation
website: www.danadeclaration.org

Forest Peoples Programme
1c Fosseway Business Centre,
Stratford Road, Moreton-in-Marsh
GL56 9NQ
Tel +44 1608 652893
Fax +44 1608 652878
email: info@fppwrm.gn.apc.org
website: www.forestpeoples.org

OXFAM landrights resource bank (information and links on African land rights)
www.oxfam.org.uk/landrights

Tourism Concern
277-281 Holloway Road
London N7 8HN
Tel +44 (0) 20 7753 3330
Fax +44 (0) 20 7753 3331
email: info@tourismconcern.org.uk
website: www.tourismconcern.org.uk

US

American Indian Movement (AIM)
Grand Governing Council
PO Box 13521
Minneapolis, MN 55414
Tel +1 (612) 721 3914
Fax +1 (612) 721 7826
email: aimggc@worldnet.att.net
website: www.aimovement.org

Kalahari Peoples Fund
(Provides funding and technical assistance to San and other peoples of southern Africa)
4811-B, Shoalwood
Austin, TX 78756, US
Tel +1 (512) 453 8935
Fax +1 (512) 459 1159
email: kalahari@mail.utexas.edu
website: www.kalaharipeoples.org

Bibliography

This only lists key books and not reports or web-based sources, whose details are given in chapter endnotes.

John Beauclerk and Jeremy Narby with Janet Townsend, *Indigenous Peoples: A fieldguide for development* (OXFAM 1988).

Megan Biesele and Kxao Royal, *San* (The Rosen Publishing Group 1997).

Simon Broughton, Mark Ellingham and Richard Trillo (eds), *The Rough Guide to World Music* (Rough Guides 2000).

Julian Burger, *The Gaia Atlas of First Peoples* (Gaia Books Ltd 1990).

– *Report from the Frontier: The state of the world's indigenous peoples* (Zed Books and Cultural Survival 1987).

Mark Cocker, *Rivers of Blood, Rivers of Gold: Europe's conflict with tribal peoples* (Pimlico edition 1999).

Roxanne Dunbar Ortiz, *Indians of the Americas: Human rights and self-determination* (Zed Books 1984).

Andrew Gray, *Indigenous Rights and Development: Self-determination in an Amazonian community* (Berghahn Books 1997).

IWGIA, *The Indigenous World 2000-2001* (IWGIA 2001), *2001-2002* (IWGIA 2002).

Lee Miller (ed), *From the Heart: Voices of the American Indian* (Pimlico 1997).

Roger Moody (ed), *The Indigenous Voice: Visions and realities, 2 vols* (Zed Books and IWGIA 1988).

Jeremy Narby and Francis Huxley (eds.), *Shamans Through Time: 500 years on the path to knowledge* (Tarcher/Putnam 2001).

Anne Pattel-Gray, *Through Aboriginal Eyes: The cry from the wilderness* (WCC Publications 1991).

Hugo Slim with Paul Thompson, *Listening for a Change: Oral testimony and development* (Panos 1993).

Anthony Swift and Ann Perry, *Vanishing Footprints: Nomadic people speak* (New Internationalist Publications Ltd 2001).

Colin Turnbull, *The Forest People* (Pimlico edition 1993).

Kathrin Wessendorf (ed), *Challenging Politics: Indigenous peoples' experiences with political parties and elections* (IWGIA 2001).

Index

Page numbers in **bold** refer to main subjects of boxed text

Aboriginal Embassy 85, 101-2
Aboriginals 28, 33, 36, 38, 43, 46, **47**, 54, 65, 77, 79, 85, 87, 99, 102, 110, 112, 113, 114, 124, 140
Adivasis 14, 65, 109
Afghans 70
Africa 36, 37, 39-40, 83, 135, 139-40; see also under individual countries
African Initiatives 130, 140
agreements, landmark 129-30
Aguaruna 73-4
aid 57, 124, 130-2, 134
Alaska 26, 53, 86
alcoholism 78
Algeria 70, 111
Algonkians 34
American Indian Movement (AIM) 140
Amnesty International 93, 139
Amungme 126
Angola 48
anthropologists 42
Anti-Slavery International 76, 84, 126, 139
Aotearoa/New Zealand 33, 51, 57, 105
Apache 100
Arawaks 12, 32
Argentina 65
Assembly of First Nations 140
Ashaninka 74
Asia Indigenous Peoples Pact 86
assimilation of children 30, 79-80
Australia 12, 28, 30, 33, 35, 36, 46, 47, 54, 61, 65, 77, 79, 85, 89, 90, 91, 99-102, 103, 110, 112, 124, 125, 140
Awá 65
Aymara 27, 99
Bagyéli 65
Baka 109
Bangladesh 70
Barabaig 39, 63-4
Batwa 59
Belgium 37
Benin 89
biopiracy 103-7, 128
Black Power 85
Bolivia 27, 62, 99
Borneo 124
Botswana 17, 48, 122
Brazil 14, 27, 36, 49, 61, 64-6, 71, 79, 116
Britain/UK 33, 67, 84, 85, 89, 90, 95, 98, 140
British Columbia 133
Burkina Faso 130
Burma (Myanmar) 14, 27, 70, 74-5
Cambodia 59
Cameroon 65, 115
Canada 13, 30, 35, 50, 53, 55, 61, 63, 66, 72, 78, 86, 87, 97, 104, 140; see also British Columbia; Labrador and Quebec
Center for World Indigenous Studies 28, 139
Chakma 70
Champlain, Samuel de 34

Cheyenne 83
Chickasaw 39
children 75-6, 123, 128
    forcible assimilation of 30, 79-80
    suicides by **61**
Chile 65
Chin 75
China 70, 117, 134
Choctaw 38
COICA 86
collective ownership of land 28, 52-3
Colombia 49, 61, 93-4
colonialism 29-45, 134
    landmark legal cases against **96**
    treaties 98-9
Columbus, Christopher 32
community advocacy 132
conflict, effects of 66-9
Congo 31, 36, 37, 114
conservation 11, 131
Cook, Captain James 33, 44
Cooper, Dame Whina **105**
Cortés, Hernando 35
Cree 129-30, 133
Cultural Survival 139
culture iceberg **50**
Damara 54
Dana Declaration on Mobile Peoples and Conservation 140
Darwin, Charles 33, 42
dates, landmark **86**
Dayaks 65
Decade of the World's Indigenous Peoples 22-3, 86
definitions of indigenous peoples, 11-17, 19-20
Dene 50, 55
Denmark 129
development, good or bad? 120-7
Dinka 56, 70
diseases 34-7, 77-9
distribution map 21
Draft Declaration on the Rights of Indigenous Peoples 24
Dreamtime 46, **47**
Earth Summit Johannesburg 2002 see World Summit on Sustainable Development
East Timor 131
Ecuador 27, 65, 72
education 30, 40-42, **62**, 131
Efe 20
environmental knowledge 46-52
Enxet 65
European Network for Indigenous Australian Rights (ENIAR) 140
Evén 54
exhibits, live human **41**
exoticization 43-4
Fiji **94-5**
Filipinos 71
Finland 18, 129
first contact 31-4
First Peoples of the Kalahari 139
First Peoples Worldwide 126, 139
foods, wild **56-7**

Index

Forest Peoples Programme 140
France 89
Freedom Ride 99-101
Fulani 115
future prospects 132-7
Germany 39, 40, 73
Geronimo **100**
Greece 89
Greenland 26, 53, 129
Griqua 87
Guaraní 61
Guatemala 12, 86, 88
Herero 40
Herzog, Werner 73-4
Hispaniola 12, 32
HIV/AIDS 79
human remains, return of 88-9
human rights victories **90, 92**
hunter-gatherers 26-7, 42-3
Hurons 34
identification difficulties 17-18
Inca 35, 36, 52
India 17, 27, 52, 65, 70, 86, 109
Indigenous Peoples of Africa Co-ordinating Committee (IPACC) 135, 139
Indigenous Peoples Biodiversity Information Network (IBIN) 139
Indonesia 106
Innu 22, 65
intellectual property see also biopiracy 49, 107, 136
International Indian Treaty Council 86, 87, 139
International Labour Organization (ILO)14, 17, 86, 126, 139
International Work Group for Indigenous Affairs (IWGIA) 12, 86, 139
Inuit 20, 26, 53, 109
Inuit Tapiriit Kanatami 140
Iran 94
Iraq 94, 95, 96
Iroquois 12, 34, 86, 130
isolation, right to 121
Kachin 75
Kalahari Peoples Fund 140
Kanaky/New Caledonia 97-8
Karamojong 67
Karen 14, 27, 70, 74, 75
Kayapo 27, 49
Kennewick Man 91
Kenya 12, 37, 85, 91-2, 96
Kgalagadi 122
Khanty 65
Khoisan see also San 89, 127
Kikuyu 12, 135
Kimberley Declaration 127, 136
knowledge, environmental 46-52, 128, 136
Kurds 70, 76, 94-7, 112
Labrador 65
Lakota 48, 83
land and nature
 ancestral links **47**, 48
 collective ownership 28, 52-3
 loss/threats to 6, 58, 62-6, 96
 pollution **66**, 92
 respect for 5, 54, 106

spiritual links **47**, 53-5
land rights victories **90, 97, 103**, 133
land struggles 91-4, **105, 106**
languages, threats to 42, 76-7
Lapland 109
Lese 20
Maasai 10, 32, 71, 85, 96, 110, 135
Mabo, Eddie **103**
Makah 122
Malaysia 65
Mali 115
Mama Yosepha Alomang **106**
Maninka 115
Maori 36, 43, 49, 51, 54, 57, 77, 79, 87, 98, 105, 110
Mapuche 65
Mari Boine and her band 115
Mashpee 84
massacres 37-40, 66, 93
Maya 12, 35, 86
Mayagna **90**
Mbuti 20, 41, 109, 110
McGuinness, Bruce **85**
media representation 72-4
Mekranoti 109
Menchú, Rigoberta 86, **88**
Métis 20, 140
Mexico 35, 36, 62, 100
Minority Rights Group International (MRG) 14, 139
missionaries 40-2
Mohawk Nation 20
Mohegan 84
Mon 70
Montagnards 68-9
Montauk 84
Morales, Evo **99**
Morocco 70, 111
mortality rates **77**, 79
museums, return of human remains from 88-9
music 108-15
Myanmar (Burma) 14, 27, 70, 74-5
Nagas 27, 54, 70, 75
Nama 40
Nambiquara 65
Namibia 48, 54, 122
Naskapi 133
Native Americans 12, 13, 20, 35, 36, 41, 52, 53, 77, 78, 79, 89, 98, 117, 131; see also under named peoples
Ndebele 87, 135
negative representation 72-4
New Caledonia see Kanaky/New Caledonia
New Guinea 109
New Zealand see Aotearoa/New Zealand
Nicaragua 90
Nigeria 92
Nisga'a **97**, 133
nomads 26, 42-3; see also pastoralists
non-governmental organizations (NGOs) see aid
Nootka 108
Norway 18, 129
Nuer 56, 135

Index

numbers of indigenous
  peoples/societies 20
Ogiek 91-2
Ogoni **92**
Ole Gilisho, Parsaloi **96**
OXFAM 140
Paez 93, 94
Palaung 75
Paraguay 65, 79
pastoralists 25-6;
  see also nomads
Penan 124
Pende 31
Permanent Forum on Indigenous Issues
  23, 86, 136-7
Peru 62, 73
Peters, Dr Carl 32-3
Philippines 72, 120
Polynesians 36
population slumps 36
Portugal 31, 36, 37
prejudice against nomads/
  hunter-gatherers 42-3
protests (Australia) 99-102
Quebec 34, 65, 129-30, 133
Quechua 27
racism 41, 73, 99, 100, 120
refugee crises 69-70, 75
representation in media 72-4
research 80-2
resistance movements 83-107
resistance music 111-13
respect for natural world 5, 54, 106
Riel, Louis **104**
rights, indigenous 11, 18, **22-3**, **24**, 127
Rio Declaration 86
Rohingya 70
Roma 28, 43, 70
romanticism 58-9
Rousseau, Jean-Jacques 44
Saharawi 70, 111-12
Samburu 85
Sami 18, 109, 115
San 17, 20, 41, 48, 65, 71, 80-2, 118-19,
  122-3
Sanema 48
São Tomé and Príncipe 37
Sechelt 133
self-determination 13, 15-17, 132-4
self-rule
  legislation **133**
  struggles 94-8
Senegal 115
shamanism 53, 100, 115-19
Shan 75
Siberia 54, 65, 76, 117-18
singing see music and shamanism
Sioux **116**
slavery 36, 37, 74-6, 83
Somali 26
Songhai 115
Soto, Hernando de 31-2
South Africa 87, 122, 127
South African San Institute (SASI) 139

Spain 31, 35, 36
spending on indigenous programs **125**
spiritualism 53-5;
  see also shamanism
Stanley, Henry Morton 38
subsistence farmers 27-8, 48-9, 52
Sudan 56-7, 75-6
suicides by children **61**
Survival International 65, 82, 122, 139
sustainable ways of living 25-8, 48-9, 52
Swazi 87
Sweden 18
Syria 94
Tahiti 35, 36, 44
Taino 32
Tanzania 10, 63-4, 71, 131
Tasmania **38**, 39, 89
terrorism, measures against 67, 95
Tibet 134
tourism, effects of 10-11, 70-2
Tourism Concern 70, 140
treaties 97
  colonial 98-9
Tribal and Indigenous Council (India) 86
tribal peoples 13, 14, 19
Truganini **38**, 89
Tuareg 115, 130
tuberculosis **78**, 79
Tukano 49
Turkey 76, 94, 112
Udege 65
Uganda 67
unemployment rates **72**
United Nations' initiatives 14, 15, 17, 22-5
United States 13, 20, 30, 32, 35, 61, 67,
  83, 84, 90, 91, 96, 98, 128, 140; see
  also Alaska
urbanized indigenous people 56-8
Venezuela 48
Vietnam 68-9
Wampangoags 35
West Papua 65, 106, 111, 126
Western Sahara 111
Western Shoshone 137
Wichí 65
wild foods 48, **56-7**
women 27, 55-6, 60-1, 75-6, 123, 124,
  128
Working Group of Indigenous Minorities
  in Southern Africa (WIMSA) 80, 122,
  140
Working Group on Indigenous
  Populations 86
World Bank 16-17
World Council of Indigenous Peoples 19,
  22-3, 58, 86, 87
World Music 113-15
World Summit on Sustainable
  Development (WSSD) 127-9
Yanomami 14, 64-6, 79
Yothu Yindi 114
Zap Mama 114-15
Zimbabwe 55, 87